THOMAS GRAY

A LIFE IN LETTERS

Bill Roberts

With happy memories
of shared sessions
in the music room

Bill

Northern Academic Press
2016

First published in 2016 by Northern Academic Press
(Second edition, corrected and illustrated)

British Library Cataloguing in Publication Data: a catalogue record for this book is available from the British Library.

ISBN No. 0-9528103-3-9

Set in WordPerfect X8 in Perpetua 12 / 11 / 10 pt and Goudy Old Style 12 pt.in PDF format.

Printed and Bound in the European Union by Martins of Berwick.

To The Cosmoba
A slice of Italy in London
Close enough to where Gray used to live
Cherishing good food in the way Gray used to do
And not too far from The British Library

Two poets:
one of skied, and inward personal, ode,
and elegy - lyrist of arrowy stress,
the filtered phrase: the other unacknowledged
poet of field and wood, flower, temperatures
and weathers; whose eye incised appearance
and behaviour with ageless, lucid
words. Another man who used
to notice such things.

From *For Thomas Gray* by Alastair Macdonald

La biographie de Gray est enfermée dans sa correspondence
– Roger Martin

Thomas Gray

Woodcut by H.G.Andrews, 1948

CONTENTS

ACKNOWLEDGEMENTS

The acknowledgements page of any book is a useful guide to the thoroughness of its preparation. In this case I have to confess that I have received little or no help in writing this book. The book has developed from a long-term study of Gray's letters as collected in the three volumes of the *Correspondence of Thomas Gray* (edited by Paget Toynbee and Leonard Whibley, Oxford: Clarendon Press, 1935), and from multiple and various essays written about him, and, most importantly, from following Gray on the ground as he travelled round the country. My most constant and reliable guide, both in detailed comment and in establishing attitudes and approaches, has been Roger Lonsdale's edition of the poems (*The Poems of Thomas Gray, William Collins, and Oliver Goldsmith*, Longman, 1969), which is as near perfect as can be, supported by Professor Lonsdale's lecture to the British Academy, published as *Thomas Gray: versions of the Self*.

TEXTUAL NOTE

The text of Gray's letters has been set up from Toynbee and Whibley's *Correspondence of Thomas Gray*, using Gray's punctuation and orthography: starting sentences without a capital letter, using abbreviations for "which" (w^{ch}), and using a symbol for the long 's' (ʃ), when a double 's' occurs mid-syllable.

Some material in this book is repeated from my earlier book, *Thomas Gray's Journal* (Northern Academic Press 2012): from the Introduction to that book and from the chapters on the Tour in the Highlands and the Tour in the Lakes.

PREFACE

Gray presents a challenge to any biographer. The letters provide a fund of useful and reliable information but there is little else in the way of contemporary evidence on which to build. Edmund Gosse (Macmillan 1909), who knew how to write, took a breezily independent line, filling in gaps with assumptions that he couldn't prove, not much interested in psychology or sex, but what he writes is very readable. Robert Ketton-Cremer's biography (Duckworth 1935) also reads well but is short, particularly brief about the poems, and avoids any real problems, like the relationships with West, Walpole, or Bonstetten. Lytton Sells's work (Allen & Unwin 1980) is downright annoying, because of its constant *animus* against Gray; one would think that a requirement for any biographer would be to like his subject but Lytton Sells plainly thinks that Gray is an over-rated poet and a selfish and unkind man in personality. Robert Mack's fairly recent biography (Yale UP 2000) is excellent in most of the ways that one could desire, scholarly, well researched, and, in this case, particularly good on the poems. Better than all these, however, is Roger Martin's *Essai sur Thomas Gray* (OUP Paris). Written in French in 1934 and difficult to come by – out of print, hardly available even in academic libraries, and rarely to be found in second-hand book lists – it is still worth the effort of finding a copy, for it is written with flair and imagination and is the only biography to give a vivid sense of what the man was probably like. Knowing my own limitations in imaginative creativity, I have not tried to compete; I have tried instead to use the letters to bring up topic after topic, aspect after aspect of Gray's life and character. The result is a different kind of biography: not following an uninterrupted time-line, not trying to fill in every minute of every day. It also results in a different view of Gray: a subdued personality of warmth and kindness, a mind of astonishing quickness and range, an incomplete life, that might have married (or relaxed into a deeper personal relationship), might have written more and greater poems, might have written about the countryside he so much enjoyed travelling through, might have contributed more to the sciences of natural history.

The Font at St. Michael's, Cornhill

where Thomas Gray was baptized

[Photograph by the author]

INTRODUCTION

Thomas Gray was born in Cornhill in London on 26th December, 1716, the fifth child of Philip Gray, a scrivener, and of Dorothy Gray, née Antrobus. According to the standard biographies, Dorothy had eleven children but the others all died at various stages of childhood, Thomas being the only survivor. According to the parish registers for St Michael's, Cornhill, however, Dorothy had only ten children, of two of whom there is no further record, presumed died young. Of the other eight, two (besides Thomas) in fact survived beyond a few months. A first Philip lived to the age of three years and a second Philip lived a similar span. The father, Philip Gray, had previously been married and had had two children by the first marriage. Both these children and, of course, the wife had died. These details are worth elaborating because they make clear the appalling surroundings of repeated births, sicknesses and early deaths by which Thomas's childhood was surrounded and the guilt which he may have felt as the only survivor, or at least the insecurity and fear. This fact, of which the standard biographies make little, is surely crucial. At one crisis of health in his childhood Gray apparently suffered a fit, from which he was allegedly only saved by his mother's opening a vein with her scissors, "by that means relieving the determination of the blood to the brain" (according to the nineteenth-century biographer, Edmund Gosse). In fact, though blood-letting was an accepted practice at the time, Mrs Gray may well have done more harm than good. It is more than ever a miracle that Thomas survived, his febrile convulsions perhaps indicating some inherited weakness. We also know that Gray's father was violent and abusive towards his wife. By 1735, after 25 years of marriage, the situation was so bad that Gray's mother applied to a Dr John Audley for legal advice on the possibility of taking action in the courts against her husband. The complaint was that "almost ever since he hath been married, he hath used her in the most inhuman manner, by beating, kicking, punching, and with the most vile and abusive language". What Dorothy Gray appeared also to be afraid of was that her husband had the long-term intention of driving her out of her business with her sister as a milliner. It would appear that she relied on this business to finance Thomas at school and that she received no financial support from her husband. The law at that time was of no help to her, since Dr Audley reported back that the most the courts would be prepared to tolerate was a separation and that this would be only in extreme circumstances. How extreme did they have to be, one wonders? Thomas's childhood must therefore have been unhappy, violent, insecure, made tolerable only by the love of his mother, for whom he not surprisingly developed a strong and close affection, and by the care of his mother's brothers, Thomas and Robert Antrobus. It is hard to think of a major writer with a less promising childhood.

At the age of eleven Thomas Gray was sent to school at Eton College, at his mother's expense. One might have thought that the apparently slight, quiet Gray would have had a hard time of it but the reverse was true: he thrived. Perhaps as an *oppidan* (a lodger in the town) he experienced a less strict discipline; perhaps he was lucky in his boarding house. The life of a colleger was proverbially strict and harsh and Gray recommended to his friend, Wharton, in a letter in 1761, that he sent his son to Eton as an *oppidan*, so that he might avoid "the hardships of College". The teaching, at least in the classics, must have been excellent, and he lived in a protected world of congenial friends. There may well be an element of idealization in Gray's re-creation of that "careless childhood" in the *Eton College* ode but he clearly looked back on those days as a time of happy innocence, swimming, playing trap-ball, walking along the river-banks, clearly not taking part in the rougher traditions of those times, such as hunting the ram. He became a member of a close-knit, supportive group of four friends, the other three being Richard West, Thomas Ashton, and Horace Walpole. Gray's friendship with the Keats-like figure of West was particularly close and passionate, though his friendship with Walpole, the son of the Prime Minister, was more important to him socially and in his later literary life. Gray went up to Cambridge as a pensioner (one who pays his own expenses) at Peterhouse in 1734, Walpole following (to King's) in 1735.

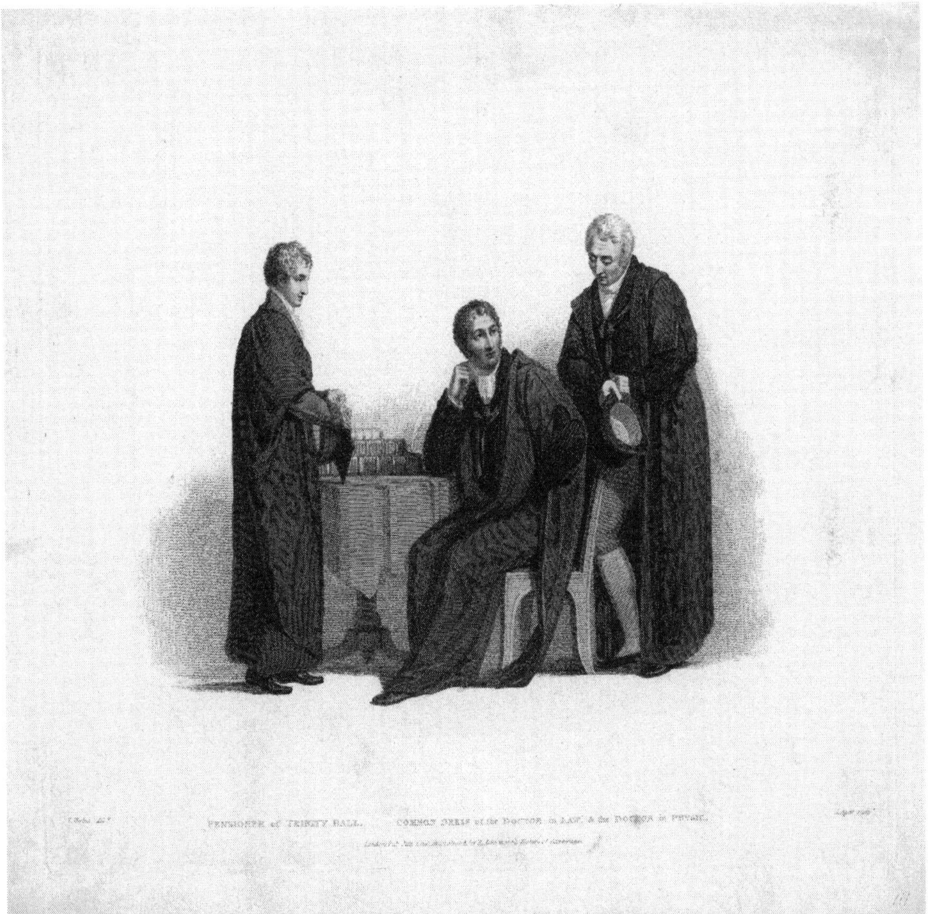

Cambridge Academic Dress

CHAPTER ONE

1734 Until July: At school, Eton College.
4 July: Entered at Peterhouse, Cambridge.
October onwards: At Peterhouse, **Cambridge.**

Gray had some difficulty in leaving his schooldays behind, in shedding his boyish enthusiasms and irresponsibilities, in casting off old connections and striking out and making new ones. In July 1734 he left Eton and the Quadruple Alliance broke up, and he was faced with an unfamiliar world. He was at first entered at Pembroke College Cambridge on 4th July but quickly switched to his uncle Antrobus's college, Peterhouse. Walpole, Gray's prop or role model, as the phrase now is, went up to London for the winter and did not appear at Cambridge (King's) until March of the following year. West, Gray's closest friend on an emotional level, was sent, with or without his consent, to Christchurch, Oxford. Ashton, a more distant member of the once-close group, arrived at King's in September and was quickly absorbed into the company of other Old Etonians. From October Gray resided in lonely isolation at Peterhouse, from where, at the end of October 1734, he wrote this letter to Walpole.

> For God's sake send me your Quaere's, & I'll do my best to get information upon those Points, you don't understand: I warrant you imagine that People in one College, know the Customs of others; but you mistake, they are quite little Societies by themselves: ye Dreſses, Language, Customs &c are different in different Colledges: what paſses for Wit in one, would not be understood if it were carried to another: thus the Men of Peterhouse, Pembroke & Clare-hall of course must be Tories; those of Trinity, Rakes; of Kings, Scholars; of Sidney, Wigs; of St Johns, Worthy men & so on: now what to say of this Terra Incognita, I don't know; First then it is a great old Town, shaped like a Spider, with a nasty lump in the middle of the it, & half a dozen scambling long legs: it has 14 parishes, 12 Colledges, & 4 Halls,

these Halls only entertain Students, who after a term of years, are elected into the Colledges: there are 5 ranks in the University, subordinate to the Vice-chancellour, who is chose annually: these are [Masters, Fellows, Fellow-Commoners, Pensione]rs, & Sizers; The Masters of Colledges are twelve grey-hair'd Gentlefolks, who are all mad with Pride; the Fellows are sleepy, drunken, dull illiterate Things; the Fellow-Com: are imitatours of the Fellows, or else Beaux, or else nothing: the Pension: grave formal Sots, who would be thought old; or else drink Ale, & sing songs against y[e] Excise. The Sizers are Graziers Eldest Sons, who come to get good Learning, that they may all be Archbishops of Canterbury: these 2 last Orders are qualified to take Scholarships; one of which, your humble Serv[t] has had given him: first they led me into the hall, and there I swore allegiance to y[e] King; then I went into a room, where I took 50000 Latin Oaths such as, to wear a Square Cap, to make 6 Verses upon the Epistle or Gospel every Sunday morning, to chant very loud in Chappel;, to wear a clean Surplice, &c: &c: Now as to eating: the Fellow-Com: dine at the Fellows Table, their Commons is worth 6s-4d a-week, the Pensioners pay but 2s-4d; if anybody don't like their Commons, they send down into the kitchen to know what's for Sizing: the Cook sends up a Catalogue of what there is; and they chuse, what they please: they are obliged to pay for Commons, whither they eat it, or no; there is always Plenty enough: the Sizers feast upon the leavings of the rest; as to Dreſs, the Fell:Commoners usually wear a Prunella Gown with sleeves, a hat & no band: but their proper habit has its sleeves trimmed with Gold-lace, this they only wear at publick Ceremonies; neither do the Noblemen use their pr: Habit commonly, but wear only a black Padesoy Gown: the Men of Kings are a sort of University by themselves; and differ in Customs from

> all the rest; everybody hates 'em & when Almanzor[1] comes to me, our People stare at him, like a Lord-mayors show, & wonder to see a human creature among them....

Gray was still only 16 years old, nearly 17 it is true, when he wrote this letter. What breathes through it, is the brashness of youth tempered by a precocious wit; it gives evidence, nevertheless, of an eye for satire and of some liberal prejudices, all hidden beneath a shy, conservative, conformist temperament. He had been in Cambridge only a few weeks when he made this devastating survey of the eighteenth-century university; not surprisingly there are some mistakes and misrepresentations within an otherwise enjoyably Hogarthian picture.

It is quite true that eighteenth-century Cambridge was sleepy and 'unreformed' and Gray certainly reflects that state. Colleges were lucky to get more than three or four freshmen each year and even luckier if they included titled young gentlemen. The ladder of advancement had not yet acquired its fixed status of public school to university to government. One looks in vain through the list of admissions for famous scientists, generals, or politicians, though the young William Pitt did follow Gray to Pembroke much later in 1773. The Senior Common Room was not full of eager intellectuals busily researching their specialities, though the fellows may not have been as decadent as Gray describes, 'sleepy drunken dull illiterate things'. These comments may be dismissed as jejune but some of Gray's first impressions are nevertheless interesting. Like any fresher he was fascinated by the gowns and the different status they conferred. Like a poet-to-be he describes them accurately with resounding adjectives - 'prunella' and 'padesoy'[2]. Full academic dress is part of the initial excitement of going to university - and still is. Different colleges still do have slightly different gowns at Cambridge. They do also have their different

---

[1] The Quadruple Alliance name for Thomas Ashton, probably given him because he had acted the part of Almanzor, a character in Dryden's *Conquest of Granada*, in a performance at Eton.

[2] 'Padesoy' - 'a strong corded or gros-grain silk fabric much worn in the eighteenth century' (OED).

reputations, though it is curious that Trinity, which is now so grand and up-market, should have been seen in the eighteenth-century as the home of rakes and ne'er-do-wells. Gray also reflects the climate that prevailed at that time of undisciplined riot among some undergraduates, drinking the night away and staggering into the street posts in the morning. Winstanley quotes a 1749 incident when two fellow-commoners of Trinity were convicted of being at an inn until 4 o'clock on Sunday morning and then going to the Market Cross and 'in riotous manner eating lobsters and drinking wine there'[3]. Winstanley was writing in 1922 and what he saw as riotous behaviour may not be construed as such now.

The fact that Gray was awarded a scholarship was more than just a tribute to his academic ability; it was worth £10 and, as Gray's entire Hall charges for his first year only amounted to £14.8s. 8½d., it made a significant contribution to his income as a student, supported with difficulty by a mother, deserted by her husband.

Gray eventually found life at Cambridge un-fulfilling but it became his 'home', his base for a restless life. His biographers do not seem to have come to terms with the fact that Gray spent his life in two rooms, a bedroom and a living room. He never had a home in which he could spread himself. He complains in a later letter of not having a garden, just a few plants on a window-sill. He seems, however, to have acquired books in profusion and must have lined his room with bookcases. He was interested in music and may have had a keyboard of some sort. He was also interested in food and must have found some way of cooking, some way of practising the receipts that he collected. Over the years he did collect a small band of friends, mostly based on Cambridge contacts: Richard Stonehewer, William Cole, Thomas Wharton, John Chute, and James Brown. As one surveys this list, it is notable how many were, like Gray himself, lonely men, with no fixed purpose in life, struggling with an unhelpful eighteenth-century social system to find a role for the independent searcher, enquirer, and writer. Cambridge did also provide him with a base, but for intellectual challenge, he had to retreat into his books and into his own mind.

---

[3] D.A. Winstanley, *The University of Cambridge in the Eighteenth Century*, Cambridge U.P., 1922, p.16.

***Susannah Cibber**, drawn by John Faber, 1714-36*

CHAPTER TWO

1735	July: Cambridge
	July to October: London
	October: Cambridge
	November: Admitted at Inner Temple.
1736	January: **London**

By the beginning of January 1736, Gray had been at Cambridge for a full year. Much of what he did in that time, is lost; without Walpole and the support of new friends, Gray was directionless. He had to make up his mind about a career and had been entered in the previous November at the Inner Temple, with the objective of a career in the law. While he prevaricated about a future career, he amused himself. In January of 1736 he went up (or 'down') to London to sample its pleasures. From there he wrote this letter to Horace Walpole:

> I can't tell whither our situations are much changed, since this time twelvemonth; certain I am however, that there is a great alteration: I don't succeed to your diversions in town, I believe, & yet am absent from Cambridge without regret, nay with pleasure, tho' not infinitely happier here: - I have very little to tell you, as to the place, call'd London:- Adriano[4] expired a few days ago, & his auncient Predeceſsour Artaxerxes[5] succeeds him for the present, wch I think to visit tonight: the Town (in submiſsion to your

[4] *Adriano* was an opera at the King's Theatre in the Haymarket performed several times in December 1735.

[5] *Artaxerxes* was an opera announced for performance at the King's Theatre on 10 January, after this letter.

judgement) don't much admire Delane[6]; Mrs Porter[7] acts in ye Albion Queens, but I shall stay for another Play, before I see her; neither have I much inclination for old Cibber in Sr Courtly Nice[8], nor for young Mrs Cibber[9] in Voltaire's Zara[10], in wch she performs the principal part for ye first time of her appearance in that way: I went to King Arthur last night, which is exceeding fine; they have anew man to supply Delane's place, one Johnson, with ye finest person & face in the world to all appearance; but as awkward, as a Button-maker; in short, if he knew how to manage his Beauties to advantage, I should not wonder, if all the Women run mad for him: the inchanted part of the play, is not Machinery, but actual magick: the second scene is a British temple enough to make one go back a thousand years, & really be in ancient Britain: the songs are all Church-musick, & in every one of ye Chorus's Mrs Chamber sung ye chief part accompanied with

Roaring, Squawlings, & Squeakations dire.

---

[6] Dennis Delane (d. 1750), an Irish actor, who began his career in Dublin, coming to London in 1730.

[7] Mary Porter (d. 1765) was the leading lady on the London stage, after the retirement of Mrs Oldfield in 1730.

[8] Sir Courtly Nice, the lead part in John Crowne's successful comedy (1685). '...in *Sir Courtly Nice* he (Crowne) did achieve a significant contribution to the company of memorable Restoration fops and to the rising tide of essentially moralizing comedy'(*The Revels History of Drama in English*, V, p. 206.

[9] Susannah Cibber, sister of the composer Thomas Arne, wife of actor Colley Cibber. In 1736 Cibber made her début as a dramatic actress in the title role of Aaron Hill's *Zara,* with great success.

[10] *The Tragedy of Zara* is a five- act tragedy in verse by Voltaire. The play was widely performed in Britain well into the 19th century in an English adaptation by Aaron Hill and was the inspiration for at least thirteen operas.

Mrs Giffard is by way of Emmeline, & should be blind, but, heaven knows! I would not wish to see better than she does, & seems to do; for when Philidel restores her to sight, her eyes are not at all better than before; she is led in at first, by a Creature, y^{t} was more like a Devil by half, than Grimbald himself; she took herself for Madame la Confidente, but everybody else took her to be in the Circumstances of Damnation: when Emmeline comes to her sight, she beholds this Mrs Matilda first, & cries out

Are Women all like thee? Such glorious Creatures!

wch set the people into such a laugh, as lasted the whole Act: the Frost Scene is excesʃive fine; the first Scene of it is only a Cascade, that seems frozen; with the genius of Winter asleep & wrapt in furs, who upon the approach of Cupid, after much quivering, & shaking sings the finest song in the Play: just after, the Scene opens, & shows a view of arched rocks covered with Ice & Snow to ye end of ye Stage; between the arches are upon pedestals of Snow eight Images of old men & women, that seem frozen into Statues, with Icicles hanging about them & almost hid in frost, & from ye end come Singers, viz: Mrs Chambers, &c: & Dancers all rubbing their hands & chattering with cold with fur gowns & worsted gloves in abundance; there are several more beautiful Scenes; but rather than describe 'em, I ought to beg pardon for interrupting your happineʃs so long, and conclude myself,

your poor Servant ever
TG

Two points of interest emerge from this letter. The first is Gray's lack of direction at this stage of his life. He was clearly disillusioned with Cambridge, or saw that it was not leading him in the direction that he wanted. In the letter he describes trying the life of a man-about-town, copying Horace Walpole perhaps, but, although he indulges himself, he doesn't seem to want that either. Perhaps what he wanted was what he afterwards got: a life devoted to literature or, if that is too much of a generalization, a life in which he could read, write, study, think - and somehow be paid for it. Most of us only get that kind of life, reduced to cognitive reflection, when we retire.

What also emerges is an interesting picture of eighteenth-century dramatic experience. It was an era when the stage was very active but producing mediocre plays or operas for a very badly behaved audience. Gray in his account here gives a quick trip round the London theatre scene in 1736: the plays and operas on show and the leading actors and actresses: Dennis Delane and Susannah Cibber, Mary Porter and an unidentifiable Mrs Chambers. Indoor theatres were experimenting with spectacle and Gray was obviously taken with the illusion of a winter scene: frost, ice, snow, actors shivering in their winter clothes. It is on a par with Folies Bergères spectaculars, or at least as I remember them from the fifties. *King Arthur* was an exception to the mediocrity: a semi-opera, with fine music by Purcell and libretto by Dryden. What Gray watched was the 1736 revival of a play/dramatic opera first seen in 1691. It is an extremely interesting piece, occasionally revived in concert or in dramatic form. Its plot is based on the opposition of King Arthur's Christian Britons to the pagan Saxons and in places it has resemblances to *The Tempest*. The lead part of Emmeline was played by a Mrs Giffard, wife of the theatre manager, Henry Giffard, but it was the singing of Mrs Chambers that really attracted Gray; he was clearly impressed with Cupid's aria, ("What power art thou...") in the Frost scene. Mrs Chambers would later score a great success as Polly Peachum in *The Beggar's Opera*. No sign, however, that Gray reacted when the shepherdesses reminded the shepherds that, 'a little after toying/Women have the shot to pay'. Gray remained keen on music throughout his life, learning the piano and collecting scores of composers and operas that he liked. Later on in the year, in July, Gray went to another opera, this time Handel's *Atlanta*, again staged as a spectacular, but this time with accomplished singers in the persons of Gioacchimo Conti, a famous soprano, and Anna Strada, a soprano also imported from Italy by Handel as a member of his company.

What is disappointing about Gray's comments on *King Arthur* is their superficiality. With the exception of his enthusiasm for Cupid's song, which is, indeed, a fine piece still, he fails to react in a meaningful way to the opera as a work of art. The audience may well have been amused by Emmeline's unconvincing blindness but that is surely a triviality, the kind of schoolboy silliness one gets impatient with. Not every-one agrees, however, that this is a triviality. Michael Burden felt strongly enough to comment: 'In an age when verisimilitude was not always high on a London theatregoer's list of desiderata, it is encouraging to find such absurdities the subject of ridicule'. This reaction in any case did not affect the work's popularity and it ran for an astonishing 35 nights, not just as the usual main piece - that is, as the main work on a program that included a short afterpiece - but as the only piece on the program. Further, these nights were consecutive; the work was too popular on its initial run to be "in repertory"[11]. More importantly, however, he makes no comment on the beauty of Purcell's music or on whether the play/opera has anything to say about patriotism or national spirit. A modern writer analyses the Frost scene as 'an allegorical expression of Emmeline's supposed sexual frigidity'[12]. There is no sign that Gray reacted to the play/opera at that level. Gray would not get a job as music critic on a modern quality newspaper. Readers would be looking for more balance and more depth to the comments.

What is going on here is particularly interesting in the context of the history of opera. Who has the greater importance, the librettist or the composer? In this work Dryden had to face up to the pre-eminence of the music: 'he shifts to being a collaborator in writing a libretto for a composer' (*Revels* V, p.291). There was a contest going on between a native British art-form, dramatic opera, and imported Italian opera, which eventually triumphed. 'In practice, a dramatic opera was a full-scale theatrical entertainment, organized as a five-act drama, including one production number to each act' (*Revels* V, p. 292). Listening to *King Arthur* today on disc, as [almost] the only means by which one can now encounter the old art-form, it is difficult not to feel a wish to return to it.

Gray was capable of a more appreciative, more empathetic appreciation of musical performance but we have to wait some years before we find the kind of enthusiastic involvement with a production in the most unlikely of places. Perhaps Gray in the following letter, written nearly thirty years later, was trying to impress Algarotti with the broad-mindedness that had come with age.

---

[11] See Burden, in *Restoration: Studies in English Literary Culture 1660-1700*, 34,1-2, pp.117-138)]

[12] Curtis Price, *Notes to English Concert Orchestra* CD recording, 1992.

> I cannot help telling you, that eight or ten years ago, I was witneſs to the power of your comic musick. there was a little troop of Buffi, that exhibited a Burletta in London, not in the Opera House, where the audience is chiefly of the better sort, but on one of the common Theatres full of all kinds of people and (I believe) the fuller from that natural aversion we bear to foreigners: their looks and their noise made it evident that they did not come hither to hear; and on similar occasions I have known candles lighted, broken bottles, and pen knives flung upon the stage, the benches torn up, the scenes hurried into the street and set on fire. the curtain drew up, the music was of Cocchi, with a few airs of Pergolesi interspersed. the singers were (as usual) deplorable, but there was one girl (she called herself Niccolina) with little voice and leſs beauty; but with the utmost justneſs of ear, the strongest expreſsion of countenance, the most speaking eyes, the greatest vivacity and variety of gesture. her first appearance instantly fixed their attention; the tumult sunk at once, or if any murmur rose, it was hushed by a cry for silence. her first air ravished everybody; they forgot their prejudices, they forgot, that they did not understand a word of the language; they entered into all the humour of the part, made her repeat all her songs, and continued their transport, their laughter, and applause to the end of the piece.
>
> *[From a letter to Count Algarotti, dated September 9th, 1763 (Cambridge)]*

This is the voice of a man who could distinguish the essential qualities of art or literature or scenery that made life worth living, that made experiences significant, those moments in the theatre when you forget about your surroundings in involvement with the emotion evoked on stage.

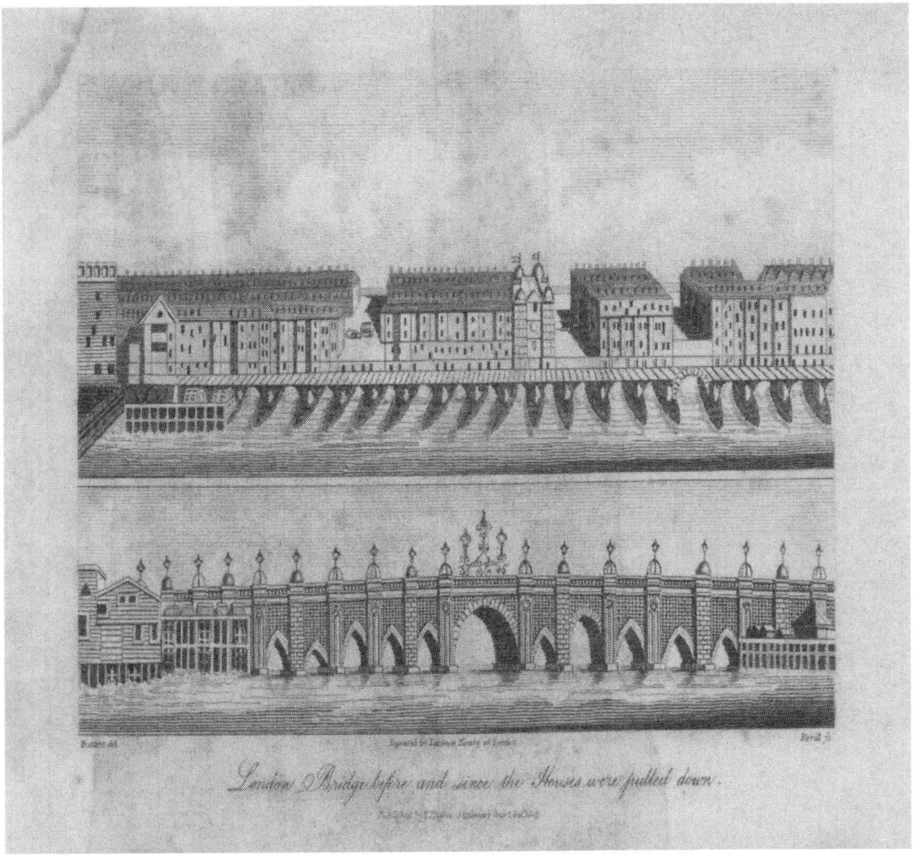

London Bridge, Before and After the houses were pulled down.

CHAPTER THREE

1736 **February: *Dr Audley's Opinion***
January to February: Cambridge
February: Sarah Gray dies and leaves Gray her property
February to March: London
March to June: Cambridge
May: *Hymeneal* *on the Marriage of the Prince of Wales*
June to October: London and Burnham
October to the following July: Cambridge

One of the assumptions of this book is that the letters give the whole story about Thomas Gray. This is not always true and there are two instances in 1736 where some important historical or personal information has to be inserted. The first of these instances is the obtaining by Mrs Gray in February 1736 of the legal opinion of Dr Audley on her complaint about her husband's conduct. As has already been mentioned in the Introduction, this was not to Mrs Gray's advantage. Dr Audley reported pessimistically about Mrs Gray's chances of obtaining a separation on grounds of cruelty. Dr Audley's opinion was that 'This was a most unhappy case, and such a one, as I think, if possible, should be referred to, and made up by some common friend; sentences of separation, by reason of cruelty only, being very rarely obtained'. No common friend seems to have emerged and no action seems to have been taken. One would think that Philip Gray had been handed a trump card and yet the complaints of cruelty appear to cease and Thomas Gray appears to have returned to being on good speaking terms, or at any rate to being on passable corresponding terms, with his father. This was clearly an important episode on Thomas Gray's life and yet we have no solid information about its consequences.

Equally important at about the same time was the death of his aunt, Sarah Gray, Philip Gray's younger sister. Somewhat surprisingly, she chose to leave her estate to her nephew Thomas and not to her brother. This estate comprised a number of houses on London Bridge, the value of which must have been considerable. Gray appears to have been able to sell these properties in a short space of time and to invest the proceeds. In the future he would have an income, probably not great but enough live on. Gray never lost the concern he had grown up with about money and his notebooks are full of short entries about the cost of everyday necessities. This bequest must have made a huge difference to Gray. Whether one goes on to speculate, as Mack does, on a change in mental attitude is another matter. 'Gray probably felt that his situation was now somehow more respectable, more fitting, and even - finally free of some slight and lingering shame'. Most people who come up from humble origins in my experience have tougher mental outlooks.

At the same time, 1736, Gray was beginning to miss Richard West, his closest acquaintance at Eton, a man of similar mental outlook, charitable, warm in his affections, someone in whom he could confide. West (1716–1742) was the only son of Richard West (c.1691–1726, lawyer, playwright, and politician) and Elizabeth Burnet (1692–1748). In youth he was described as being 'tall and slim, of a pale and meagre look and complexion'[13] and Mason spoke of his genius as being 'more brilliant than his friend's'. While the rest of his school friends went to Cambridge, West, as we have seen, was sent to Oxford, matriculating at Christ Church on 22 May 1735 at the age of nineteen. So West at this time was studying in Oxford and Gray was trying to exist without company at Peterhouse.

None of Gray's letters beside this one, written to Richard West from Cambridge in December, 1736, give such a vivid picture of his being, in the modern sense of the term, completely fed up. Fed up with Cambridge. Fed up with life generally. Uncertain of where to go or what to hang on to, except friendships.

> You must know that I do not take degrees, and, after this term, shall have nothing more of college impertinencies to undergo, which I trust will be some pleasure to you, as it is a great one to me. I have endured lectures daily and hourly since I came last, supported by the hopes of being shortly at full liberty to give myself up to my friends and claſsical companions, who, poor souls, though I see them fallen into great contempt with most people here, yet I cannot help sticking to them, and out of a spirit of

[13] According to William Cole, a contemporary at Eton, quoted in *Correspondence of Thomas Gray*, OUP, 1935, Vol. 1, footnote 6 to page 28.

obstinacy (I think) love them the better for it; and indeed, what can I do else? Must I plunge into metaphysics? Alas, I cannot see in the dark; nature has not furnished me with the optics of a cat. Must I pore upon mathematics? Alas, I cannot see in too much light; I am no eagle. It is very poſsible that two and two make four, but I would not give four farthings to demonstrate this ever so clearly; and if these be the profits of life, give me the amusements of it. The people I behold around me, it seems, know all this and more, and yet I do not know one of them who inspires me with any ambition of being like him. Surely it was of this place, now Cambridge, but formerly known by the name of Babylon, that the prophet spoke when he said, 'the wild beasts of the desert shall dwell there, and their houses shall be full of doleful creatures, and owls shall build there, and satyrs dance there; their forts and towers shall be a den for ever, a joy of wild aſses; there shall the great owl make her nest, and lay and hatch and gather under her shadow; it shall be a court of dragons; the screech owl shall rest there, and find herself a place of rest. You see here is a pretty collection of desolate animals, which is verified in this town to a tittle, and perhaps it may also allude to your habitation, for you know all types may be taken by abundance of handles; however, I defy your owls to match mine.

If the default of your spirits and nerves be nothing but the effect of the hyp, I have no more to say. We must all be subject to that wayward Queen; I too in no small degree own her sway, I feel her influence while I speak her power. But if this be a real distemper, pray take more care of your health, if not for your own at least for our sakes, and do not so soon weary of this little world: I do not know what refined friendships you may have contracted in the other, but pray do not be in a hurry to see your acquaintance above; among your terrestrial familiars, however, though I say it that should not say it, there positively is not one that has a greater esteem for you than....Yours most sincerely, &c.

Of all his friendships, the one with West was the closest and the most confiding. West's own poetry is inevitably scarce but one poem, *Ad Amicos*, written in 1736, makes very clear the degree to which he was missing his Eton friends at this time. It also allows us to make some judgement on his ability as a poet, inferior to Gray maybe but intimately confederate with him:

> YES, happy youths! on Camus' sedgy side
> You feel each joy that friendship can divide,
> Each realm of science and of art explore,
> And with the ancient blend the modern lore,
> Studious alone to learn whate'er may tend
> To raise the genius or the heart to mend;
> Now pleas'd along the cloister'd walks you rove,
> And trace the verdant mazes of the grove,
> Where social oft' and oft' alone ye chuse
> To catch the zephir and to court the Muse;
> Mean-time at me (while all devoid of art
> These lines give back the image of my heart)
> At me the pow'r that comes or soon or late,

Whether the friendship between the two was or became homosexual, we shall never know now; some modern critics choose to think so. But West, though at a distance, was the one person to whom Gray could speak in trust. Not completely openly because even here some of what he says is in code, a code protected by a mockery use of the Old Testament and its most minatory prophet, Isaiah. In fact, Gray put up with Cambridge for two more years. He may speak dismissively of West's 'default of spirits' and of his own disillusion as 'nothing but the effect of the hyp' but this was an affliction that was to dog himself, as well as West, throughout his life, a peculiarly eighteenth-century affliction in its common-ness among major and minor literary figures.

Horace Walpole

CHAPTER FOUR

1737	From previous October to July: Cambridge
	July to November: London
1738	Previous November to April: Cambridge.
	April - May London
	May - September: Cambridge
	September onwards: London

Of Gray's other friendships, the one with Horace Walpole was clearly the longest-lasting, the most influential. The style of this letter to him, written from Cambridge on March 7thth, 1738, is dictated by the pose Gray feels he has to strike towards him, by the impression of smartness and shared knowing-ness that gave an artificiality to their relationship.

> Thank God, I had a very good night's rest, and am sufficiently awake to answer your letter, tho' likely to be more dull, than you that write in your sleep: and indeed I do not believe, that you are ever so much asleep, but you can write to a relation, play a sober game at Picquet, keep up a *tete á tete* conversation, sell a bargain, or perform any of the little offices of life with tolerable spirit; certain I am, that there are many people in the world, who in their top spirits are no better *eveillés* than you are at four in the morning, reclined upon your pillow. I believe, I partly gueſs [what is] your hopeful branch, I fancy you may find the first letters of both somewhere between H & T inclusive; if I interpret your hieroglyphs aright. as to my journey to London, which you are so good as to preſs, alas! what can I do? if I come , it is for good & all, & I don't know how it is, I have a sort of reluctance to leave this place, un-amiable as it may seem; 'tis true Cambridge is very ugly,

she is very dirty, & very dull; but I am like a cabbage, where I am stuck, I love to grow; you should pull me up sooner, than anyone, but I shall be ne'er the better for transplanting: poor Mr Cornwallis[14] is here, sadly alter'd, so that one can hardly know him; Towers still stands out, & refuses to admit him; so that they have called in their visitours[15], that is the Vice-chancellour, Dr Bently[16], & Dr Ashton[17]; but nothing is yet determined: the Aſsizes are just over, I was there; but I a'nt to be transported: Adieu,

yours sincerely, T: Gray

The letter sheds an interesting light on Horace Walpole's personality. Extroverted, lively, sociable: the reverse of everything we can see in Gray himself, so that one wonders what drew the two together. Walpole secured an intelligent and obedient audience, a willing follower, a connoisseur of the arts; Gray obtained an entry to the highest levels of society, some financial assistance towards the costs of a leisured way of life, and a witty listener to his own word-making. If that sounds too selfish on both sides, it is worth balancing these debts with the credit of enjoying each other's company, tested over a long period of time, in youth and into middle age.

What we need, to counter-balance this letter of Gray's to Walpole, is a letter from Walpole to Gray but only one such letter survives from these early

---

[14] Afterwards Archbishop of Canterbury. 'Poor' because he had suffered a stroke of palsy.

[15] The role of visitors was to adjudicate. The visitors for Christ's were the Vice-Chancellor and two senior doctors of divinity.

[16] Dr Richard Bentley, Master of Trinity, 1700-42.

[17] Dr Charles Ashton, Master of Jesus College, 1701-1752

years, a ponderous and lengthy letter written by Walpole in October 1735, describing his journey from London to Cambridge by way of a parody of Addison's *Travels in Italy*. It gave him the opportunity of indulging their mutual enjoyment of Virgil's *Aeneid* but the joke is laboured and contributes little to our knowledge of their respective personalities.

One other way of sensing the emotional climate of the relationship is to compare one of Walpole's letters to Richard West at this time, since Walpole's attitude to West was very similar to his attitude to Gray. Walpole wrote to West from Cambridge in November 1735 to console West by suggesting in effect that he was not missing much by being out of things at Oxford.

> We have not the least poetry stirring here; for I can't call verses on the 5th of November and 30th of January by that name, more than four lines on a chapter in the New Testament is an epigram. Tydeus rose and set at Eton: he is only known here to be a scholar of King's. Orosmades and Almanzor are just the same; that is, I am almost the only person they are acquainted with, and consequently the only person acquainted with their excellencies. Plato improves every day: so does my friendship with him. These three divide my whole time though I believe you will guess there is no quadruple alliance: that was a happiness which I only enjoyed when you was at Eton. A short account of the Eton people at Oxford would much oblige, my dear West.

Walpole writes with polite affection and some egotism: 'I am almost the only person they are acquainted with'. It is inevitably a backward-looking letter, cherishing the days of their friendship at Eton, the days of the 'quadruple alliance' of Walpole, Ashton, West and Gray, with their code-names of Orosmades (Gray) and Almanzor (Ashton); Tydeus must have been another Eton acquaintance, not identified. Walpole comes across at this time as the dominant personality, witty but with a juvenile propensity to elaborately imagined situational games.

Assessments of Walpole's personality by the few academic writers who have focussed on Walpole's life vary in intensity but share some features of eccentricity in common. Timothy Mowl's assessment of Horace is guarded. 'He was a notably effeminate bachelor with a strong vein of malice in his writing: but if he had homosexual tendencies, he appeared to have been too fastidious ever to have given way to them.'[18] Mowl goes on to describe the importance of the early friendships at Eton. 'It was with the members of the Quadruple Alliance that Horace was most closely engaged in the years immediately after leaving Eton, and what emerges from their correspondence is that the College had been a very happy and successful educational environment. Its pupils loved what they had learnt, they liked or loved each other, and they continued to express that affection through the same passages of wit and classical reference that had been standard class-room practice.'

W.S. Lewis, who was a less sweeping biographer than Mowl, quoted Walpole's own assessment of his character. "Walpole," he said of himself, "had a warm conception, vehement attachments, strong aversions; with an apparent contradiction in his temper - for he had numerous caprices, and invincible perseverance....He had great sense of honour, but not great enough, for he had too much weakness to resist doing wrong, though too much sensibility not to feel it in others".[19] His character in Lewis's partial view, shines out of his letters as ebullient and spontaneous, with the wealth and social position to do much good and a little harm.

Yet another assessment of Horace Walpole, more recent but more colourful, is that of George Haggerty in an American academic journal: '....what the letters reveal is a bitchy, playful, arrogant, self-satisfied, intriguing, acquisitive, loving, and devoted friend who loves deeply and long

---

[18] Tmothy Mowl, *Horace Walpole: The Great Outsider*, London: faber & Faber, 1996, p.2

[19] W.S.Lewis, *A Guide to the Life of Horace Walpole*, Yale.U.P., 1973.

and devotes himself to his house and his collections with the same kind of energy he puts into friends and (sometimes) politics. This is the person who emerges so vividly and richly in the letters that he himself preserved for posterity: isn't it enough?' [20]

Horace Walpole played an important and, for a time, controlling part in Gray's life. In 1739 he made the life-enhancing Grand Tour possible and then, later, after the reconciliation and recovery from the quarrel in Reggio, he became, as it were, Gray's literary agent, encouraging and directing the publication of his poems. This is the material for a later chapter in this biography, when Walpole's role changes, and there will be letters of a very different tone and content. At this early stage of his life Gray certainly needed Walpole for psychological support.

Walpole now has these three claims on our attention: as a collector, as the inventor/creator of Strawberry Hill, and as one of the greatest of eighteenth-century letter-writers. Bruce Redford compares Walpole's gift for 'the converse of the pen' to 'the ormolu mounts with which the French encrusted their delicate Chinese porcelain.....' Walpole's letters belong to 'a minor category of rococo decorative arts'. Gray was one of Walpole's noteworthy correspondents, 'taking delight in playing witty games', contributing to the games and encouraging the flights of fancy.

In September 1738 Gray left Cambridge, and took up his abode in his father's house for six months, apparently with no definite plans regarding his own future career. It was Horace Walpole who stepped in and solved this crisis in his life's direction.

---

[20] George Haggerty *Studies in English Literature 1500-1900* (Rice University), Vol. 46, no.3, pp.543-562, 2006.

The Three-Horse Post-Chaise: A scene near Amiens,
Print by F.G.Byron, 1791

CHAPTER FIVE

1739	January to March: London
	March 29 to April 4 (NS): Began Grand Tour
	April - June : Paris
	June - September: Rheims
	Sept. 7-15: Journey to Lyons
	Sept. 13 to Oct. 31: Lyons, with excursion to Geneva
	Oct. 31 to Dec. 16: Grande Chartreuse Turin Florence.
1740	21-25 March: Journey to Rome
	25 March to 4 July: Rome, Tivoli, and Naples
	July 4-7: Journey to Florence
	July to following April : Florence (over-winter)
1741	April 24 – 3rd May: To Bologna & Reggio (Quarrel)
	May -July: Venice.
	July to September: Journey via Padua, Chartreuse, Paris to London.

According to Gosse, 'in September 1738 Gray left Cambridge...apparently with no plans ...but out of this sleepy condition of mind he was suddenly awakened by Horace Walpole's proposition that they should start together on the grand tour. The offer was a generous one: Walpole was to pay all Gray's expenses, but Gray was to be absolutely independent....' The two travellers set off from England in April 1739 and journeyed for eighteen months across France and Italy, apparently with no definite plan other than that of reaching Rome ultimately, and Naples possibly as a furthest south. The main cities visited in fact turned out to be: Paris, Rheims, Dijon, Lyons, [then across the Alps by the Mont Cenis pass], Turin, Genoa, Parma, Modena, Bologna, Florence, Rome and Naples, returning via Florence. Gray wrote fairly frequently to his mother, also to his father, and to Richard West; he also kept a journal of his tour beginning in Rheims. The first of these letters was to his mother from Amiens on April 1st, 1739, a few days after his arrival in France.

> As we made but a very short journey today, and came to our inn early, I sit down to give you some account of our expedition. On the 29th (according to the style here) we left Dover at twelve at noon, and with a pretty brisk gale, which pleased everybody mighty well, except myself who was extremely sick the whole time; we

> reached **Calais** by five: The weather changed, and it began to snow hard the minute we came into the harbour, where we took the boat, and soon landed. Calais is an extremely old, but very pretty town, and we hardly saw any thing there that was not so new and so different from England, that it surprized us agreeably. We went the next morning to the great Church, and were at high Maſs (it being Easter Monday). We saw also the Convent of the Capuchins, and the Nuns of St. Dominic; with these last we held much conversation, especially with an English Nun, a Mrs. Davis, of whose work I sent you, by the return of the Pacquet, a letter-case to remember her by. In the afternoon we took a Post-chaise (it still snowing very hard) for Boulogne, which was only eighteen miles further. This chaise is a strange sort of conveyance, of much greater use than beauty, resembling an ill-shaped chariot, only with the door opening before instead of the side; three horses draw it, one between the shafts, and the other two on each side, on one of which the postillion rides, and drives too: This vehicle will, upon occasion, go fourscore miles a day, but Mr. Walpole, being in no hurry, chooses to make easy journeys of it, and they are easy ones indeed; for the motion is much like that of a sedan, we go about six miles an hour, and commonly change horses at the end of it: It is true they are no very graceful steeds, but they go well, and through roads which they say are bad for France, but to me they seem gravel walks and bowling greens; in short it would be the finest travelling in the world, were it not for the inns, which are mostly terrible places indeed.

If Gray had a family send-off from London as he began his Grand Tour, he doesn't say so. Perhaps it is a twentieth-century expectation. Sir Robert Walpole would have had other things on his mind and was probably not over-anxious over his wayward son Horace, while Mrs Gray probably preferred to keep out of the way of Thomas's high society friends. The two young men must have travelled down to Dover by post-chaise and boarded the regular mail packet boat. These were small single-masted ships, which could do the crossing in a matter of hours but which, with a contrary wind, could take days. On the open deck it was a rigorous experience and the delicate Gray spent his time being sick. Arrival in Calais would not be the end of the ordeal, as Turner's painting of *Entering Calais Harbour* makes clear. It often involved transfer to a small boat and a soaking in a high sea before one reached the safety of the jetty.

It is interesting to compare the beginning of Gray's Grand Tour with Patrick Leigh Fermor's account of his first steps on the other side of the channel as a young man in 1933. Fermor's writing is certainly more exciting and far more detailed but both share a sense of the newness of everything in the alien world across the sea. Where Fermor noticed, 'the roadside calvaries and the twinkle of sanctuary lamps in the churches', Gray sees 'on every hillock a windmill, a crucifix, or a Virgin Mary dressed in flowers'. It is Catholic Europe which strikes one most strangely after Protestant England.

By April 4th the two tourists had reached Paris. They spent two months in Paris, visiting other British ex-pat's and going to theatres and concerts. They then moved on to Rheims and spent three months there. On the 7th September, the two Grand Tourists left Rheims, and reached Dijon three days later. They spent four days there, admiring the then-newly-built Palais des Etats and strolling in the city's symmetrically laid-out park and fascinated by the rotunda of the then-Abbey-Church (now the Cathedral) of St Benigne. On the 18th of September they reached Lyons, and this town became their headquarters for the next six weeks. From there, the friends set out on an excursion across the mountains, in the course of a visit to Geneva, in order that they might visit the Grande Chartreuse. This impressed Gray so forcibly by the solitary grandeur of its situation that its impact requires separate consideration in the following chapter.

> After their visit to the Chartreuse in November, the two, still friends, set out to cross by the Mont Cenis Pass into northern Italy. This was another extraordinary experience, bringing them face to face again with wild nature, and so it also requires separate consideration, out of chronological sequence, along with the visit to the Chartreuse, in the following chapter.

Once firmly in Italy, the country of classical splendour they had come to see, Gray began his relentless search of the galleries for great paintings. The interests of the two began to divide at this point, as Gray worked hard at seeing all that there was to see and Walpole amused himself in a more sociable manner. Gray's tastes were those of the eighteenth century: the primitives were yet to be discovered and Caravaggio was too lively for his nerves. Guido Reni would always move him, and in the Church of St Ambrosio in Genoa he found a marvellous *Assumption*, with 'the Virgin in a bright heaven above with vast beauty and devotion in the face...' In Parma it was Correggio that captivated him, not surprisingly, in the dome in the cathedral, even if it was at that time 'in sad condition'. He made detailed and sometimes captious notes as he went. In Bologna he examined Raphael's *St Cecilia* at considerable length. 'This celebrated picture to me does not seem to merit all it's fame.' And then there followed a criticism of the regularity with which five figures are placed in the painting, 'which savours a good deal of Gothicism'. Florence and Rome, however, brought out the superlatives: Parmegiano's *Madonna del Collo longo* (in the Palazzo Pitti in Florence) being 'inexpressibly fine' and 'lovely beyond imagination'. Gray's favourite painting in all the multiplicity of choice available to him in Rome was probably Guido Reni's *Rape of Helen* in the Palazzo Spada, which earned the tribute, 'the most lovely and Guidesco imaginable'. He visited all the major galleries and most of the churches, great and small, as well as going out to the catacombs along the Appian Way, clambering down the claustrophobic tunnels, despite his alleged timidity. Walpole was already beginning to tire of this assiduous, pernickety inspection.

Two events sparked noteworthy episodes in the letters from Rome. One of them was a visit to St Peter's for a procession to venerate St. Veronica's handkerchief. Gray describes his reactions, suitably muted for his mother's sensibilities, in a letter to Mrs Gray, dated Good Friday, 1740.

> It was something extremely novel to see that vast church, and the most magnificent in the world, undoubtedly, illuminated (for it was night) by thousands of little crystal lamps, disposed into the figure of a huge croſs at the high altar, and seeming to hang in the air. All the light proceeded from this, and had the most singular

effect imaginable as one entered the great door. Soon after came one after another, I believe, thirty proceſsions, all dreſsed in linen frocks, and girt with a cord, their heads covered with a cowl all over, only two holes to see through left. Some of them were all black, others red, others white, others party-coloured; these were continually coming and going with their tapers and crucifixes before them; and to each company, as they arrived and knelt before the great altar, were shown from a balcony at a great height, the three wonders, which are, you must know, the head of the spear that wounded Christ; St Veronica's handkerchief, with the miraculous impreſsion of his face upon it; and a piece of the true croſs, on the sight of which the people thump their breasts, and kiſs the pavement with vast devotion. The tragical part of the ceremony is half a dozen wretched creatures, who with their faces covered, but naked to the waist, are in a side-chapel disciplining themselves with scourges full of iron prickles; but really in earnest, as our eyes can testify, which saw their backs and arms so raw we should have taken it for a red satin doublet torn, and shewing the skin through, had we not been convinced of the contrary by the blood which was plentifully sprinkled about them.......

The second incident concerns the exiled Stuarts, whom Gray and Walpole saw during their visit to Rome. Gray dutifully wrote to his father as requested; one wonders if Walpole had more covert communication with his father, the prime minister.

The Pretender (whom you desire an account of) I have had frequent opportunities of seeing at church, at the corso, and other places; but more particularly, and that for a whole night, at a great ball given by Count Patrizii to the prince and princeſs Craon (who were come to Rome at that time, that he might receive from the hands of the Emperor's minister there the order of the golden fleece) at which he and his two sons were present. They are good

> fine boys, especially the younger, who has the more spirit of the two, and both danced inceſsantly all night long. For him, he is a thin ill-made man, extremely tall and aukward, of a most unpromising countenance, a good deal resembling King James the Second, and has extremely the air and look of an idiot, particularly when he laughs or prays. The first he does not often, the latter continually. He lives private enough with his little court about him, consisting of Lord Dunbar[21], who manages every thing, and two or three of the Preston Scotch lords, who would be very happy to make their peace at home.

Gray is extremely unguarded in his comments, especially risky in view of the widespread practice of opening letters and censoring them. His implied optimism about the security of the Hanoverian regime is also remarkable, in view of the fact that within a few years one of the 'good fine boys' would be within reach of London at the head of a Jacobite army. Gray did not write to his father often, about five times in all, and his tone is always distant and respectful.

From Rome the two journeyed south to Naples. They remained in Naples for about three weeks and saw most of the tourist sites. They were moderately venturesome and indeed experienced more difficulties and dangers than most of Gray's present-day academic critics (often eager to criticize his timidity) will have done: they went down caves and tunnels, rowed across the bay, walked across the volcanic Solfatara, but did not ascend Vesuvius, which was dangerously active in the mid-eighteenth century. From Naples, towards the end of his stay, Gray sent this letter to his mother.

> Your maps will show you the situation of Naples; it is on the most lovely bay in the world, and one of the calmest seas: it has many other beauties besides those of Nature. We have spent two

[21] Lord Dunbar, the Hon. James Murray (c.1690 - 1770), second son of the fifth Viscount Stormont, titular Earl of Dunbar (1721)

days in visiting the remarkable places in the country round it, such as the bay of Baiæ and its remains of antiquity; the lake of Avernus, and the Solfatara, Charon's grotto, &c. We have been in the Sybil's cave and many other strange holes under ground (I only name them, because you may consult Sandy's travels[22]); but the strangest hole I ever was in, has been today at a place called Portici, where his Sicilian Majesty has a country seat. About a year ago, as they were digging, they discovered some parts of ancient buildings above thirty feet deep in the ground: Curiosity lead them on, and they have been digging ever since; the paſsage they have made, with all its turnings and windings, in now more than a mile long. As you walk you see parts of an amphitheatre, many houses adorned with marble columns, and incrusted with the same; the front of a temple, several arched vaults of rooms painted in fresco. Some pieces of painting have been taken out from hence, finer than anything of the kind before discovered, and with these the King has adorned his palace; also a number of statues, medals, and gems; and more are dug out every day. This is known to be a Roman town, that in the Emperor Titus's time was overwhelmed by a furious eruption of Mount Vesuvius, which is hard by. The wood and beams remain so perfect that you may see the grain; but burnt to a coal, and dropping into dust upon the least touch. We were today at the foot of that mountain, which at present smokes only a little, where we saw the materials that fed the stream of fire, which about four years since ran down its side. We have but a few days longer to stay here; too little in conscience for such a place....

---

[22] *Sandy's Travels*, 7th edition, London: John Williams, 1673, is online, with an immensely long title page, reading: 'containing an History of the original and present state of the Turkish Empire...Egypt.... The Holy Land.... and lastly Italy'. According to the Catalogue of Gray's Library in W.P.Jones, *Thomas Gray Scholar*, Harvard University Press, 1937, Gray had his own copy, which he may well have left with his mother.

What Gray is describing at the end here is the early stages of the discovery of Herculaneum; Pompeii was discovered a few years later in 1748. At this time the entry was by means of a tunnel from the Corso Ercolano. Gray described what they saw and experienced in more detail in his journal:

> The work is unhappily under the direction of Spaniards, people of no taste or erudition, so that the workmen dig, as chance directs them wherever they find the ground easiest to work without any certain view. They have been fearful of the earths falling in, & with reason, for it is but soft & crumbling, so that the paſsage they have made, is but just sufficient for one person to walk upright in. I believe, with all its windings it is now a good mile in length & every day is increasing. One descends conveniently to the depth of about 30 feet by the stone Steps of a Theatre, that they have found. They have found an *Olla* [jar] with Rice & Dates in it. the first I saw none of, but they say it retained its hardneſs. The latter was black as the wood; & of a firmer consistence.

The situation is now very different, in that the entry from the Corso Ercolano is no longer in existence, but some details remain: the jar with the dates and rice, for example, is still there to be seen in the Naples Archaeological Museum.

Gray's interest in classical literature and history took him round the Bay of Baiia to Capo Miseno and then inland to Cumae. On the way, he went through the Crypta Neopolitana, damaged during the Second World War and no longer open. He visited the Solfatara, the area where there are fumaroles, or jets of steam emerging from the ground, and did the customary visit to the Grotta del Cane (Charon's grotto, in Gray's phrase). In the latter a layer of carbon dioxide covers the floor, and it used to be the tourist trick that a dog was made to lie on the ground and be brought to the edge of extinction, then to be brought to life again outside the cave. At least Gray made strenuous efforts to revive the dog. Lake Avernus was on the way to Cumae, interesting to Gray as the entry to the underworld, interesting also as having been connected with the Lago Lucrino by Agrippa as a way of creating a safe military harbour.

Gray and Walpole went nowhere new, nowhere that was not already on an established tourist track but they were energetic: they walked considerable distances on rough tracks, they took a boat across the bay right round the headland to a point near Avernus, they ventured down some rough and ready tunnels, to locate the Grotta del Sybilla for instance. Their reactions were intelligent and measured. Gray was clearly moved by the experience of bringing classical history and literature to life.

From Naples the tourists went back to Florence and over-wintered there until the following April, in 1741. On 24 April they left Florence and went to Reggio, where they quarrelled. The probability is that Walpole made some disparaging remark about Gray, which got under his skin. Gray could take no more and he left for home on his own. He travelled north to Venice, then to Padua, Verona, and Milan.. Fortunately, he re-crossed the Alps via the Mont Cenis and came down into France by the Grande Chartreuse, which he re-visited, leaving a beautiful Alcaic ode in Latin in the Visitors' Book [see Chapter Six]. If Gray was in elegiac mood by the time he reached The Chartreuse, it cannot be a surprise, with the Tour in ruins behind him and his friendship ended in rancour. There is something of the Country Churchyard Elegy in the air and feeling of this poem. His father died within a few weeks of his return to England in September of 1741. In the October of that year he returned to Peterhouse as a Fellow-Commoner.

Vue de l'entrée de la Grande Chartreuse,
Print by J.F. Albanis de Baumont, 1787

CHAPTER SIX

1739 October: Visit to the Grande Chartreuse
November: Crossing the Mont Cenis pass.

Gray had two experiences of wild scenery while on the Grand Tour, which are quite different from what happened on the rest of the tour, two experiences which it is convenient to take out of chronological order.

Walpole and Gray travelled from Paris to Rheims and then to Dijon and Lyons, and while at Lyons they made a lengthy excursion to Geneva. They took the longest road through Savoy, that they might visit the Grande Chartreuse on the way. The solitary grandeur of its situation impressed Gray greatly and he wrote this letter to his mother on October 13th on his return to Lyons.

> It is a fortnight since we set out from hence [Lyons] upon a little excursion to Geneva. We took the longest road, which lies through Savoy, on purpose to see a famous monastery, called the grand Chartreuse, and had no reason to think our time lost. After having travelled [two] days very slow (for we did not change horses, it being impoſsible for a chaise to go post in these roads) we arrived at a little village, among the mountains of Savoy, called Echelles; from thence we proceeded on horses, who are used to the way, to the mountain of the Chartreuse: It is six miles to the top; the road runs winding up it, commonly not six feet broad; on one hand is the rock, with woods of pine-trees hanging over head; on the other, a monstrous precipice, almost perpendicular, at the bottom of which rolls a torrent that sometimes tumbling among the fragments of stone that have fallen from on high, and sometimes precipitating itself down vast descents with a noise like thunder, which is still made greater by the echo from the mountains on each side, concurs to form one of the most solemn, the most romantic, and the most astonishing scenes I ever beheld: Add to this the strange views made by the craggs and cliffs on the other

hand; the cascades that in many places throw themselves from the very summit down into the vale, and the river below; and many other particulars impoſsible to describe; you will conclude we had no reason to repent our pains. This place St. Bruno chose to retire to, and upon its very top founded the aforesaid convent, which is the superior of the whole order. When we came there, the two fathers, who are commiſsioned to receive strangers, (for the rest must neither speak one to another, nor to any one else) received us kindly; and set before us a repast of dried fish, eggs, butter and fruits, all excellent in their kind, and extremely neat. They preſsed us to stay the night there, and to stay some days with them; but this we could not do, so they led us about their house, which is, you must think, like a little city; for there are 100 fathers, besides 300 servants, that make their clothes, grind their corn, preſs their wine, and do everything among themselves: The whole is quite orderly and simple; nothing of finery, but the wonderful decency, and the strange situation, more than supply the place of it. In the evening we descended by the same way, paſsing through many clouds that were then forming themselves on the mountain's side.

Gray also wrote to West, much later in Turin in November, about this visit and some of that letter is also worth quoting, to emphasize the effect that the visit had on Gray.

In our little journey to the Grande Chartreuse, I do not remember to have gone ten paces without an exclamation, that there was no restraining: Not a precipice, not a torrent, not a cliff, but is pregnant with religion and poetry. There are certain scenes that would awe an atheist into belief, without the help of other argument. One need not have a very fantastic imagination to see spirits there at noon-day: You have Death perpetually before your eyes, only so far removed, as to compose the mind without frighting it. I am well persuaded St. Bruno was a man of no

> common genius, to choose such a situation for his retirement; and perhaps should have been a disciple of his, had I been born in his time. You may believe Abelard and Heloïse were not forgot upon this occasion: If I do not mistake, I saw you every now and then at a distance among the trees....

Walpole also wrote to West, even more enthusiastically, if further evidence is needed of the impact made by this expedition on the two travellers

> But the road West, the road! Winding round a prodigious mountain, and surrounded with others, all shagged with hanging woods, obscured with pines or lost in clouds! Below, a torrent breaking through cliffs, and tumbling through fragments of rocks! Sheets of cascades forcing their silver speed down channelled precipices, and hasting into the roughened river at the bottom! Now and then an old footbridge, with a broken rail, a leaning croſs, a cottage, or the ruin of a hermitage! This sounds too bombast and too romantic to one that has not seen it, too cold for one that has. If I could send you my letter post between two lovely tempests that echoed each other's wrath, you might have some idea of this noble roaring scene, as you were reading it....

To replicate the visit, you now need a car and a day to spare in the neighbourhood of Chambèry. Twenty or so kilometres to the south of this town is the town of Les Échelles, where Gray spent the night, and some distance further down the D520 a metalled road leads up through a narrow gorge to the Monastery of the Grande Chartreuse. The road has been much improved and it is possible to drive without difficulty and with no sensation of danger to the enclosed plateau on which the monastery is built. The road by which Gray travelled was much more primitive. He had to leave his comfortable chariot behind at Les Échelles and proceed on horseback, a rough way of proceeding that he was always reluctant to adopt. At various points the old road is still to be seen clinging to the cliff-sides, clearly un-nervingly narrow and with a few of the old bridges still surviving. It is possible to stop half-way up and walk down sections of the old road and one quickly feels a sensation of narrowness and height and river noise such as makes Gray's excited impression, as described in a letter to his mother, totally believable.

This is one of the great moments of dawning awareness, of epiphany, when Gray realized his contact with the sublime: a religious moment in that it is a realisation of unity with the natural universe. Gray never forgot this moment. It shaped everything that he wrote about and thought about later. And it is a fascinating emotion, if that is what it is, which it is difficult to analyse. One essential ingredient is fear. Gray was certainly frightened on that narrow mountain road on his way up to the Grande Chartreuse. It was narrow and there was a steep cliff on one side and a big drop on the other. He felt the vertigo. He was frightened later in life when he looked at Schiehallion on his trip to the Scottish highlands in 1765, probably because he saw in it natural forces beyond human control, as a huge dominating mass, in wild, untamed country. The fear contained a strong element of awe, of respect, of fascinated admiration. An emotion which it is only possible to feel from a position of safety, 'only so far removed, as to compose the mind without frighting it'. This was a huge discovery, because it meant that instead of being revolted and terrified by wild country, one became drawn towards it by the new feeling of heightened awe, a numinous sensation which Wordsworth and other Romantic poets would later try desperately to capture.

Gray re-visited the Chartreuse on his way home alone, and left a beautiful Alcaic ode in Latin in the visitor's book. It remains a fine poem in translation.

Some godhead haunts this harsh and holy place
(His name who knows? No petty god for sure)
Its own perennial waters grace
An abbey, its ancient woods immure.

Among the trackless crags, steep mountain-sides,
Grim peaks, by sounding torrents, forest-gloom,
More truly, know, a god resides
Than should some Phidian statue loom,

Glowing in gold and marble, under roof
Of fragrant timbers. Greetings, O good Lord,
That hauntest this wild place aloof
And if in prayer I strike a chord

Acceptable, then let me find my peace,
Young and yet weary, here. If jealous Fate
Withholds for now my longed release
And thrusts me back to things I hate,

To crowds and noise; then grant me in full age
That I may win some corner, far from strife,
And there, as in an hermitage,
Contentedly conclude my life[23].

If Gray was in elegiac mood by the time he reached The Chartreuse for the second time, it cannot be a surprise. By that time his Tour was in ruins behind him and his friendship with Walpole had ended in rancour. There is consequently something of the Country Churchyard Elegy in the air and feeling of this poem.

[23] This poem was translated into English verse for me by the late Canon Walter Ewbank, a classicist and a poet in his own right.

Gray also experienced awe, that mixture of fear and fascination that was to excite him and inspire his later travels in Scotland and the Lake District, when crossing the Mont Cenis pass into Italy. The Mont Cenis pass is not much used now but was then the normal route from France down into northern Italy. Gray's experience of the crossing is described in a letter to his mother written shortly after his arrival in Turin in November 1739.

> The winter was so far advanced, as in great measure to spoil the beauty of the prospect, however, there was still something fine remaining amidst the savageneſs and horror of the place: the sixth we began to go up several of these mountains; and as we were paſsing one, met with an odd accident enough. Mr Walpole had a little fat black spaniel, that he was very find of, which he sometimes used to set down, and let it run by the chaise side. We were at that time in a very rough road, not two yards broad at most; on one side was a great wood of pines, and on the other a vast precipice; it was noon-day, and the sun shone bright, when all of a sudden, from the wood-side, (which was as steep upwards as the other part was downwards) out rushed a great wolf, came close to the head of the horses, seized the dog by the throat, and rushed up the hill again with him in his mouth. This was done in leſs than a quarter of a minute; we all saw it, and yet the servants had not time to draw their pistols, or do anything to save the dog. If he had not been there, and the creature had thought fit to lay hold of one of the horses; chaise, and we, and all must inevitably have tumbled above fifty fathoms perpendicular down the precipice. The seventh we came to Lanslebourg, the last town in Savoy; it lies at the foot of the famous Mount Cenis, which is so situated as to allow no room

> for any way but over the very top of it. Here the chaise was forced to be pulled to pieces, and the baggage and that to be carried by mules: We ourselves were wrapped up in our furs, and seated upon a sort of matted chair without legs, which is carried upon poles in the manner of a bier, and so began to ascend by the help of eight men. It was six miles to the top, where a plain opens itself about as many more in breadth, covered perpetually with very deep snow, and in the midst of that a great lake of unfathomable depth, from whence a river takes its rise, and tumbles over monstrous rocks quite down the other side of the mountain. The descent is six miles more, but infinitely more steep than the going up; and here the men perfectly fly down with you, stepping from stone to stone with incredible swiftneſs in places where none but they could go three paces without falling. The immensity of the precipices, the roaring of the river and torrents that run into it, the huge crags covered with ice and snow, and the clouds below you and about you, are objects it is impoſsible to conceive without seeing them; and though we had heard many strange descriptions of the scene, none of them at all came up to it. We were but five hours performing the whole, from which you may judge of the rapidity of the men's motion....

Napoleon came a few decades later and engineered a much better road, climbing in gradual zig-zags to the summit; later still an English company built a short-lived mountain railway; and then came the Fréjus tunnel. Now you can drive easily to a pleasant inn at the top of the climb, call in at a museum of early travel on the summit plateau, and still find traces of the early paths that descended so steeply on the Italian side. Addison crossed in December 1701 'after a very troublesome journey'. Boswell crossed without being too perturbed, though he did admit that 'the prospect was grand' and stopped to drink the snow. Turner, however, travelling back to England nearly a hundred years later (in 1819) had a serious accident, in which the diligence overturned and caught fire. In his depiction of the scene, he clearly tried to convey a sense of the fear of elemental forces [*vide* British Museum Database]. The road is still seasonally closed in winter. To avoid these problems. a very smart train now leaves Paris every morning, providing a much quicker route to Italy for the modern Grand Tourist. It travels at high speed through uninteresting northern France, improving in scenic quality as it goes beside the lake at Annecy, disappearing into a long tunnel, and emerging into alpine Italy north of Turin. A smooth and civilized way to travel that Gray would have enjoyed.

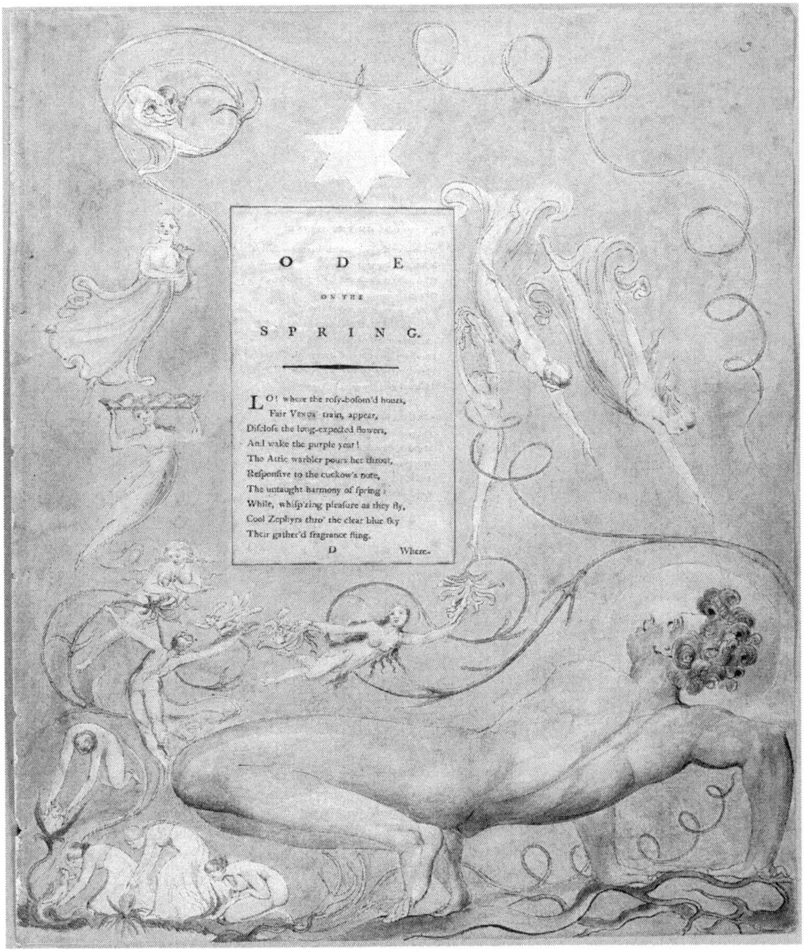

Blake's Design for the Ode to Spring

Chapter Seven

1741	24 April to 3 May: To Bologna and Reggio (**Quarrel)**
	May to July: Venice
	July to September: Journey by Mont Cenis and Chartreuse to London.
	September onwards: London.
1742	Until April: London
	May to June: Stoke
	[June 1st: Richard West died]
	June to July: London
	July to October: Stoke and London
	October onwards: Cambridge

Gray spent the winter of 1741/42 in London, much of it in the company of Richard West. As his first literary sally in the English language, he tried to write a verse drama, *Agrippina*, inspired probably by what he had seen of French drama when in Paris and making use of his knowledge of classical literature. One scene of it survives but most admirers of Gray would be prepared to accept Gosse's estimate of it as 'a false start' and move on.

West seems to have decided in the spring to leave London and to stay at a house called Popes, a manor house 2 miles to the west of Hatfield in Hertfordshire, presumably for the good of his health. Gray continued to need the contact with West for inspiration and the exchange of mutual worries and concerns and there is an exchange of ten letters within the space of a couple of months. Some of these are concerned, as always, with cheering one another out of fits of depression. As early as 1736, Gray was chastising West about 'the effect of the hyp' (Dec. 1736, letter 33). A year later Gray is complaining himself that 'low spirits are my true and faithful companions' (August, 1737, letter 40). Even while away on the tour he writes to West, metaphorically, that he has struck a medal upon himself, 'and the motto Nihilissimo'. (July 1740, letter 92). In May of 1742 he wrote to West analysing his depression as 'a white Melancholy' – a good easy sort of state, as he called it, in which he lived most of his life. Gray may speak dismissively in the letter to West of 'nothing but the effect of the hyp' but this was an affliction that was to dog him himself throughout his life, a peculiarly eighteenth-century affliction in its commonness among major and minor literary figures.

The two would-be poets also used their letters to exchange literary notions and opinions. In April of 1742, Gray wrote to West, unaware of West's closeness to death, to adumbrate a few first principles of literary composition and criticism.

> You are very good in giving yourself the trouble to read and find fault with my long harangues. Your freedom (as you call it) has so little need of apologies, that I should scarce excuse your treating me any otherwise; which, whatever compliment it might be to my vanity, would be making a very ill one to my understanding. As to matter of stile, I have this to say: **The language of the age is never the language of poetry** [my bold type]; except among the French, whose verse, where the thought or image does not support it, differs in nothing from prose. Our poetry, on the contrary, has a language peculiar to itself; to which almost everyone, that has written, has added something by enriching it with foreign idioms and derivatives: Nay sometimes words of their own composition or invention. Shakespear and Milton have been great creators this way; and no one more licentious than Pope or Dryden, who perpetually borrow expreſsions from the former.

This statement, that 'the language of the age is never the language of poetry' was later to become contentious. Wordsworth reacted strongly to the idea that there should be a special kind of poetic diction. Wordsworth aimed to give 'English poetry a new linguistic integrity by returning to its native rustic roots'. In practice both writers compromised: Wordsworth purified the language of his rustics; Gray sought vitality of language by borrowing as well as by urbane artifice.

West died at Popes of 'a consumption'[24] on 1 June 1742, and was buried in the chancel of Hatfield church. Before reading of West's death, Gray sent him a letter enclosing his '*Ode on the Spring*' but the letter was returned unopened, because West had died. This letter had contained Gray's *Ode to Spring*, The last verse of which is as follows:

> Methinks I hear in accents low,
> The sportive kind reply:
> Poor moralist! And what art thou?
> A solitary fly!
> Thy joys no glittering female meets,
> No hive hast thou of hoarded sweets,
> No painted plumage to display:
> On hasty wings thy youth is flown;
> Thy sun is set, thy spring is gone -
> We frolic, while 'tis May.

This poem, included in the letter to West, and intended probably as an answer to a poem on a similar theme by West, is arguably Gray's first major poem in English, certainly the first to be published. It was sent later to Walpole in October 1746 and, probably through Walpole's agency, was printed anonymously in Dodsley's *Collection* in 1748.

What drives one's mind to poetry is probably a mixture of motives. In Gray's case, he came to poetry as an extension of schoolboy exercises in translation and adaptation. So, it is a mental exercise, akin to solving a crossword puzzle, governed by the discipline of metre, assisted by the example of previous poets and examples, widening out as the search for the right word

[24] Horace Walpole, letter to Sir Horace Mann, 24 June 1742, *Walpole, Corr.*, 17.468–9

and the exact phrase lead one on into discovering new levels of meaning and significance. This is not the kind of rambling obscurely difficult verse that decorates the pages of the contemporary TLS but a carefully crafted allusive vehicle for moralizing and philosophizing about life. As a first poem, if you come at it from this angle, this is brilliant. You can have a quote from it on a tee-shirt or on a mug, I discover, and so it must still be making its impact. The 'Attic warbler' has also made its way into the *Oxford Dictionary of Quotations*. Personally I prefer the line: 'How low, how little are the proud...' There is much to choose from.

Thomas Ashton wrote an elegy on West's death, which was printed in *The London Magazine* in June 1742. In his response to West's death, Gray wrote an English sonnet ('*In vain to me the smiling mornings shine*') and some lengthy elegiac verses in Latin, '*De principiis cogitandi*', Book Two of which is movingly addressed to West. Gray's sonnet on the death of West is arguably concerned less with West himself, than with Gray's own sense of the futility of life. It is worth quoting in full, for it is clearly the best indicator we have of Gray's deep love of West. What permeates the poem is the contrast of the joy of nature and the grief of the poet, the indifference of the outside world to his innermost feelings.

In vain to me the smiling mornings shine,
And redd'ning Phoebus lifts his golden fire:
The birds in vain their amorous descant join,
Or cheerful fields resume their green attire:
These ears, alas! for other notes repine,
A different object do these eyes require.
My lonely anguish melts no heart but mine;
And in my breast the imperfect joys expire.
Yet morning smiles the busy race to cheer,
And new-born pleasure brings to happier men:
These fields to all their wonted tribute bear;
To warm their little loves the birds complain;
I fruitless mourn to him that cannot hear,
And weep the more because I weep in vain.

The poem was criticized by Wordsworth for its poetic diction, its adoption of a stylized language remote from real feeling, a criticism understandable perhaps in terms of what Wordsworth was trying to do but not fair on Gray and misunderstanding the irony in the poem. As Roger Lonsdale argues, 'In part the diction is intended to evoke a Miltonic richness which contrasts with the barer language (approved by Wordsworth) used to describe the poet's barren spiritual condition'(Lonsdale, p.66). Arguably, Gray's feeling about West comes over more powerfully in the Latin poem *De Principiis Cogitandi*, which he finished in June 1742, after West's death. Again, it is worth quoting directly, though from the English translation:

> But you, blessed spirit, who do not need my grief, rejoice in the starry circuit of the heavens and the fire of the pure ether whence you sprang. But if, released from cares as you are, but not beyond mortal concerns, you look back with pity on once-familiar toils and are free to perceive our trivial anxieties; if, by chance, you look down from your lofty seat on the storm of human passion, the fears, the fierce promptings of desire, the joys and sorrows and the tumult of rage so huge in our tiny hearts, the furious surges of the breast; then look back on these tears, also, which, stricken with love, I pour out in memory of you; this is all I can do, while my only wish is to mourn at your tomb and address these empty words to your silent ashes.

Wordsworth could hardly complain of a lack of sincerity or deep feeling in these sad lines.

"A True Representation of Tower Hill"

on the day of the execution of the Jacobite Lords

CHAPTER EIGHT

1743	June to September: Stoke and London.
	September to July (next year): Cambridge
1744	From previous September to July: Cambridge
	July to October: Stoke and London.
	October to May (next year): Cambridge
1745	From previous October to May: Cambridge.
	May to September.: Stoke and London.
1746	To July: Cambridge
	July to October: London & Stoke (with excursion to Hampton Court)
	October: Cambridge
	November: London
	November onwards: Cambridge.

It took four years for the 'unfortunate difference' between Gray and Walpole to fade to the point of healing. What caused this difference initially is still not clear. The probability is that it started with a remark passed on by a mutual friend, which sparked anger, but the real cause must have been the unequal relationship between the two, Gray being so clearly the socially inferior. Walpole admitted as much later. The reconciliation appears to have followed on the intervention by an unknown lady, who brought the two together. Gray's own account of the ending of animosity is given in a letter to Wharton written from Stoke in November 1745.

> I am not lost: here I am at Stoke, whither I came on Tuesday, & shall be again in Town on Saturday, & at Cambridge on Wednesday or Thursday. you may be curious to know what has past. I wrote a note the Night I came, & immediately received a very civil Answer. I went the following Evening to see *the party* (as Mrs Foible says) was something abashed at his Confidence: he came to meet me, kiſsed me on both Sides with all the Ease of

> one, who receives an Acquaintance just come out of the Country, squatted me into a Fauteuil, begun to talk of the Town & this & that & t'other, & continued with little Interruption for three Hours, when I took my leave very indifferently pleased, but treated with wondrous Good-breeding. I supped with him next night (as he desired) Ashton was there, whose formalities tickled me inwardly, for he I found was to be angry about the letter I had wrote to him. however, in going home together our Hackney-Coach jumbled us into a sort of Reconciliation: he hammered out somewhat like an excuse; & I received it very readily, because I cared not tuppence, whither it were true or not. so we grew the best Acquaintance imaginable, & I set [sat] with him on Sunday some Hours alone, when he informed me of a host of Anecdotes much to my satisfaction, & in short open'd his Heart to me with that Sincerity, that I found I had still less Reason to have a good Opinion of him, than (if possible) I ever had before. Next morning I breakfasted alone with Mr W: when we had all the *Eclairciſsement* I ever expected, & I left him far better satisfied, than I had been hitherto. when I return I shall see him again. such is the Epitome of my four Days....

Gray calls this 'all the *eclaircissement* I ever expected', implying some remaining dissatisfaction on his part. It had taken four years for the pain of the original breach to have dissolved to this point. The intervening years, in which much had happened - the death of his father and of West, the composition of some of his best poems - seem to have matured Gray into greater self-confidence. Walpole later admitted that the original quarrel had been due to his own tactlessness, to an assumption of superiority towards an underling that would have been unbearable. So Gray was able to take Walpole's breezy assumption of a return to normal relations as if nothing had happened with only the mildest of self-contained annoyance - 'very indifferently pleased' - though Ashton's part in the row was clearly less easily dealt with. For Gray, he had 'still less Reason to have a good Opinion of him [Ashton] than (if possible) I ever had before'. We don't quite know what Ashton had done but the suspicion is that Gray had written to Ashton during the Tour with some remarks about Walpole's behaviour, which Ashton had then passed on to Walpole. That presumably was the trigger for the row. There are no more letters to Ashton from this point and Gray's friendship can be considered to have ended in suppressed acrimony. Walpole, however, became the recipient of Gray's poems, starting with the *Ode on the Favourite Cat*, and the encourager of Gray into public publication.

W.S.Lewis deals with this episode in his biography of Horace Walpole. He quotes Walpole's later admission that 'too fond of my own diversions, nay, I do not doubt, too much intoxicated by indulgence, vanity, and the insolence of my situation as a prime minister's son, not to have been inattentive and insensible to the feelings of one I thought below me'. Lewis goes on to describe the reconciliation, which, he declares, 'opened the way to a new and sounder friendship that lasted unbroken till Gray's death. They visited each other at Cambridge and Strawberry Hill....He [Gray] helped Walpole with many of his antiquarian projects.... Walpole on his side was responsible for the printing of nearly all of Gray's poems, which he acclaimed with 'the Walpolian drums and trumpets sounding fortissimo.'

In these middle years of his maturity, Gray could relax and fill his letters with accounts of public events, of which he was an interested and intelligent observer, or with private scandals, which he mischievously enjoyed. The first that gets lengthy treatment is the trials of the Jacobite lords in 1746. He says little at the time in 1745 about the Jacobite rebellion and the threat to London but there is not much doubt about whose side he was on. And so, when the rebellion was finally defeated and the rebels brought to book, it is not surprising that he does not show much sympathy for them. The trials were held in public and Gray describes his reactions to them in a letter to Wharton, written from Stoke in August of 1746.

> My evenings have been chiefly spent at Ranelagh & Vauxhall, several of my Mornings, or rather noons, in Arlington Street, & the rest at the Tryal of the Lords. ....what he [Kilmarnoch] said appears to leſs Advantage, when read.

Cromartie[25] (who is about the same Age a Man of lower Stature, but much like a Gentleman) was sinking into the Earth with Grief & Dejection. with Eyes cast down & a voice so low, that no one heard a Syllable, that did not sit close to the Bar, he made a short Speech to raise Compaʃsion. it is now, I see, printed; & is reckon'd extremely fine. I believe, you will think it touching & well-expreʃsed: if there be any Meanneʃs in it, it is lost in that Sorrow he gives us for so numerous & helpleʃs a Family. Lady-Cromartie (who is said to have drawn her Husband into these circumstances) was at Leicester-House on Wednesday with four of her children; the Princeʃs saw her, & made no other answer than by bringing in her own children & placing them by her; w^{ch} (if true) is one of the prettiest Things I ever heard. she was also at the Duke's, who refused to admit her: but she waited till he came to his Coach & threw herself at his Knees, while her Children hung upon him, till he promised her all his Interest could do; & before on several Occasions he has been heard to speak very mildly of Cromartie, & very severely of Kilmarnoch. so if any be spared, it will probably be the former, tho' he had a pension of 600£ a-Year from the Government, & the Order for giving Quarter to no Englishman was found in his Pocket. as to Balmerino he never had any hopes from the beginning: he is an old soldier-like Man of a vulgar Manner & Aspect, speaks the broadest Scotch, & shews an Intrepidity, that some ascribe to real Courage, & some to Brandy. You have heard perhaps, that the first Day (while the Peers were adjourned to consider of his Plea, & he left alone for an Hour & half in the Bar) he diverted himself with the Ax, that stood by him, played with its Taʃsels & tryed the Edge with his Finger: & some Lord, as he paʃsed by him, saying he was surprised to hear him alledge anything so frivolous, & that could not poʃsibly do him the least service: he

[25] George Mackenzie (1703-66), third Earl of Cromarty; he was sentenced to death but was reprieved and received a conditional pardon in1749.

answered, that as there were so many ladies present, he thought it would be uncivil to give them no Amusement. the D: of Argyle telling him how sorry & how astonish'd he was to see him engaged in such a Cause. My Lord (says he) for the two Kings & their Rights I cared not a farthing, wch prevailed: but I was starveing; & by God if Mahomet had set up his Standard in the Highlands, I had been a good Muſselman for Bread, & stuck close to the Party, for I must eat. the Sollicitor-General came up to speak to him too; & turns about to old Williamson. Who is that Lawyer, that talks to me? My L^{d}, it is Mr Murray. Ha! Mr Murray, my good Friend (says he, & shook him by the Hand) & how does your good Mother? oh, she was of admirable Service to us; we should have done nothing without her in Perthshire. he recommends (he says) his Peggy ('tis uncertain......the favour of the Government, for she has.... [I have been diverted with an Account of old Lovat in his Confinement at] Edinburgh. there was a Captain Maggett, that is obliged to lie in the Room every Night with him. when first he was introduced to him, he made him come to his Bedside where he lay in a hundred flannel Wastcoats and a furr'd Night-gown, took him in his Arms, & gave him a long Embrace, that absolutely suffocated him. he will speak nothing but French; insists upon it, that Maggett is a Frenchman & calls him Mon cher Capitaine Magot (You know *Magot* is a monkey) at his head lie two Highland Women & at his feet two Highland Men. by his Bedside is a Close-stool to wch he rises two or three times a Night, & always says, Ah, mon cher Capitaine Magot! Vous m'excuserez, mais la Nature demande que je chie![26] he is to be impeached by the House of Commons, because not actually being in Arms, it would otherwise be necesſary, that the Jury of Inverneſs should find a Bill of Indictment against him, wch it is very sure they would not do.

[26] Chier: shit, or piss.

when the Duke return'd to Edinburgh they refused to admit Kingston's light Horse & talked of their Privileges. but they came in Sword in hand, & replied, that when the Pretender was at their Gates, they had said nothing of their Privileges. the Duke rested some Hours there, but refused to see the Magistracy.

I believe you may think it full Time, that I close my Budget of Stories....

Adieu, my dear Wharton; believe me very truly Yours T. Gray.

Gray's attitude to these trials, as manifested in his comments in this letter, should excite some discussion and debate. Gosse and Ketton-Cremer, curiously, avoid any mention of Gray's attending the trials but Mack gives them some considerable space and implies some criticism. Gray, according to Mack, is 'less passionate' in his re-telling than Walpole (who also mentions the trial in his letters), and shows 'less compassion' towards Balmerino. He also implies that Gray observed the trials as some sort of enjoyable theatrical performance, applying 'the histrionic criteria of the drama' to what he watched. There is indeed an expectation, a twenty-first century expectation, that one should show pity towards men facing the death sentence. With so much sentimental approval of the 'bonnie prince' now part of popular responses to the 1745, it is also important to counter-balance these prejudices with a realization that such an expectation would not have been there in 1746, at least, not in the mind of a protestant Englishman, content with the Hanoverian monarchical settlement and still recovering from the anxiety of the threat in 1745 to the 1688 revolution. Gray's attitude is certainly dispassionate but he is aware of what is at stake.

He is perhaps on more amenable, less controversial ground with gossip and anecdote, for which he had a gift. The story about Captain Magot is a typical one. Gray's account of Balmerino's behaviour, testing the sharpness of the executioner's axe as an amusement for the ladies, with its ironic distinction between intrepidity due to natural courage and recklessness due to alcohol, is black humour indeed but not insensitive. Gray's dislike of Balmerino's uncouth Scottishness- 'of vulgar manner and aspect' - allows him to make the most of a story which others might well have found insensitive. Yet there is compassion shown towards Lady Cromarty and her children. At least that helps to make for a balanced contemporary account, full of interest. "If I had a thousand lives, I would lay them all down in the same cause".

Gray's gift for anecdote occurs over and over again in the letters. A prize specimen is the tale of Lord Peterborough's canary-bird, which is told in a letter, much later, to the Reverend James Brown in February 1761.

> And now I am telling stories, I will tell you another nothing at all to the purpose, nor relating to anybody I have been talking of.
>
> In the year 1688 my Lord Peterborough had a great mind to be well with lady Sandwich (Mrs Bonfoy's old friend). there was a Woman, who kept a great Coffee-house in Pall-Mall, & she had a miraculous Canary-Bird, that piped twenty tunes. Lady S: was fond of such things, had heard of, & seen the bird. Lord P: came to the Woman, and offered her a large sum of money for it; but she was rich, & proud of it, and would not part with it for love or money. however he watch'd the bird narrowly, observed all its marks and features, went and bought just such another, sauntered into the Coffee-room, took his opportunity when no-one was by, slipped the wrong bird into the cage, & the right into his pocket, & went off undiscover'd to make Lady Sandwich happy. this was just about the time of the Revolution; & a good while after, going into the same Coffee-house again he saw his bird there, & said, well I reckon, you would give your ears now, that you had taken my money. money! (says the Woman) no, nor twenty times that money now; dear little creature; for if your L^{p} will believe me (as I am a Christian it is true,) it has moped & moped, and never once opened its pretty lips since the day that the poor king went away!

Gray also took an interest in more serious occasions, in the behaviour of the

Duke of Newcastle (whom he disliked), in the philosophy of the Earl of Shaftesbury (which he disapproved of), in the trial of Lord Ferrers for murder (condemned and hanged), and in 1759 in the great battle of Minden. It would be a mistake to assume that the gentle poet would know nothing about the realities of warfare. In fact, Gray was able to quote sources very close to the top of government within days of the battle occurring. He knew that the battle had begun with a mistaken order but did not know then the nature of that mistake. In fact, the six regiments of infantry had received an order to march 'upon the beating of drums', which had been misconstrued to advance 'to the beating of drums'. The infantry had attacked the French cavalry head on in battle formation, against all the then known principles of warfare, and yet had defeated them. Gray knew there had been heavy losses but he also knew that it was a resounding victory and that the French general had asked his German counterpart to take care of the injured in hospital in Minden. In a letter to James Brown, dated August 9th, eight days after the battle, quoting his own private sources ('from the best hand'), he gave a fairly accurate account of the battle.

> Very early in the morning, before the Prince {Frederick] had time to make proper dispositions, they were upon him. he had only his first line formed when the battle began, and of that line the English infantry made a considerable part....the French artillery at first did terrible execution, and it was then our four regiments suffered so much, 68 of their officers (all, I think, below a captain in degree) being killed or wounded; 207 private men killed, and above 900 wounded....the Marshal [de Contades] himself....wrote a letter to the Prince to say that, as Minden must now fall into the hands of his victorious troops, he doubted not but he would treat the wounded and sick (who were all lodged there) with his usual humanity....8000 only of ye French were slain in the field, 20 pieces of cannon (16-Pounders) taken, and 12 standards.

This battle, of course, now ranks as part of the British army's oldest traditions; several regiments still celebrate Minden day. When the British infantry and artillery were first advancing to battle they passed through some German gardens and the soldiers picked roses and stuck them in their coats. In memory of this, each of the Minden regiments now marks 1 August as Minden Day. Gray knew that 'the season for triumph is at last come'. He would soon realise that the tide of the Seven Years War had turned, that the *Annus Mirabilis* had begun as other victories followed.

The Favourite Cat

After Stephen Elmer, Print by John Scott, c.1810

CHAPTER NINE

1747 To February: Cambridge ***Ode on Cat.***
May: Stoke & London ***Eton College Ode.***
May to August: Cambridge.
August to October: London, Stoke, Strawberry Hill.
October onwards: Cambridge.

In February of this year Horace Walpole asked Gray for an epitaph on one of his cats, which had recently been drowned in a goldfish bowl at his house in Arlington Street. Gray's reply was to write the following letter , and then, in the days that followed to write the poem which we now know as *Ode on the Death of a Favourite Cat*. He then sent the poem to Thomas Wharton, who seems to have had it published in Newcastle in January 1748.

> As one ought to be particularly careful to avoid blunders in a compliment of condolence, it would be a sensible satisfaction to me (before I testify my sorrow, and the sincere part I take in your misfortune) to know for certain, who it is I lament. I knew Zara and Selima, (Selima, was it? Or Fatima) or rather I knew them both together; for I cannot justly say which was which. Then as to your handsome Cat, the name you distinguish her by, I am no leſs at a loſs, as well knowing one's handsome cat is always the cat one likes best; or, if one be alive and the other dead, it is usually the latter that is the handsomest. Besides, if the point were never so clear, I hope you do not think me so ill-bred or so imprudent as to forfeit all my interest in the surviver: Oh no! I would rather seem to mistake, and imagine to be sure it must be the tabby one that had met with this sad accident. Till this affair is a little better determined, you will excuse me if I do not begin to cry: '*Tempus inane peto, requiem, spatiumque doloris.*'[27]

[27] Virgil, *Aeneid*, iv. 433-4: "I am seeking an empty time, a rest, and a space from work/pain."

Ode on the Death of a Favourite Cat Drowned in a Tub of Gold Fishes

'Twas on a lofty vase's side,
Where China's gayest art had dyed
The azure flowers that blow;
Demurest of the tabby kind,
The pensive Selima reclined,
Gazed on the lake below.

Her conscious joy her tail declared;
The fair round face, the snowy beard,
The velvet of her paws,
Her coat that with the tortoise vies,
Her ears of jet and emerald eyes,
She saw; and purred applause.

Still had she gazed; but midst the tide
Two angel forms were seen to glide,
The genii of the stream:
Their scaly armour's Tyrian hue
Through richest purple to the view
Betrayed a golden gleam.

The hapless nymph with wonder saw:
A whisker first and then a claw,
With many an ardent wish,
She stretched in vain to reach the prize.
What female heart can gold despise?
What cat's averse to fish?

Presumptuous maid! with looks intent
Again she stretched, again she bent,
Nor knew the gulf between.
(Malignant Fate sat by and smiled)
The slippery verge her feet beguiled,
She tumbled headlong in.

Eight times emerging from the flood
She mewed to every watery god,
Some speedy aid to send.
No dolphin came, no Nereid stirred:
No cruel Tom nor Susan heard
A favourite has no friend.

From hence, ye Beauties, undeceived,
Know, one false step is ne'er retrieved,
And be with caution bold.
Not all that tempts your wandering eyes
And heedless hearts is lawful prize;
Nor all that glisters gold.

Most gold fish bowls are made of glass and are round, not suitable to a cat's rear end, and modern aquaria tend to be rectangular and equipped with lights and aerating devices. I have only ever seen one gold fish bowl that fits the ideal features – made of china, decorated, with a wide cat-friendly ledge round its rim – and that is at Wallington in Northumberland. The original, much sought after by W.S.Lewis for his house of Gray treasures at Farmington, has been preserved at Strawberry Hill.

This perfect poem celebrates an elegant domesticity. It amuses with the very lightest of undertones of threat, with the most gently acceptable hints of morality. The language could hardly be more straightforward – "she tumbled headlong in" - and it hardly matters that there are borrowings from Dryden, Pope, Milton, and Virgil for the academic critic to tease out. And yet some do find fault. Johnson was troubled that the cat became a nymph, while a more modern critic has seen far darker significances. If you have a mind to see this light-hearted mock-heroic poem in a different light, it can be seen as 'an allegorical satire on women'; as giving 'a negative representation of "femaleness"', and representing 'woman as excessive, mindless, amoral consumer'[28]. This is not what has kept the poem in the popular anthologies.

[28] Suvir Kaul, *Why Selima Drowns*, PMLA 105/March 1990, pp.223-232.

Another poet at Pembroke also wrote a poem on a cat. Christopher Smart (much later) wrote entertainingly on 'my Cat Jeoffrey':

> For I will consider my cat Jeoffrey.
> For he is the servant of the Living God duly and daily serving him.
> For at the first glance of the glory of God in the East he worships in his way.
> For is this done by wreathing his body seven times round with elegant quickness.
> For then he leaps up to catch the musk, which is the blessing of God upon his prayer.
> For he rolls upon prank to work it in.
> For having done duty and received blessing he begins to consider himself.
> For this he performs in ten degrees.
> For first he looks upon his fore-paws to see if they are clean.
> For secondly he kicks up behind to clear away there.
> For thirdly he works it upon stretch with the fore-paws extended.
> For fourthly he sharpens his paws by wood.
> For fifthly he washes himself.
> For Sixthly he rolls upon wash.
> For Seventhly he fleas himself, that he may not be interrupted upon the beat.
> For Eighthly he rubs himself against a post
> For Ninthly he looks up for his instructions.
> For Tenthly he goes in quest of food.
> ....

Christopher Smart was a colleague of Gray's at Pembroke but could not have been more different, in character or in poetic style. Smart had arrived at Pembroke Hall at the age of 17 in 1740. As the Poetry Foundation on-line biography of Smart puts it, Smart 'showed little inclination to settle down to the tranquil seclusion of college life'. He drank too much and spent too much. By 1747 he was in debt and in trouble. Gray predicted, in a letter to Wharton, written in March 1747, that he 'must come to a Jayl, or Bedlam, & that without any help, almost without Pity'. Although Gray did not join in the various efforts that were made to raise money to pay off Smart's debts, he did put his name down for two books which Smart was having published by subscription. But the two poets could not stand one another. Smart is supposed to have made about Gray the following very unpleasant remark: ' Thomas Gray walks as if he had fouled his small-clothes and looks as if he smelt it.' Smart was the kind of outspoken man who could have made such a remark, and it is certainly true that Gray was so pernickety and fussy and delicate, that the remark might well have seemed to fit him. Gray's own antagonistic attitude to Christopher Smart is clear in this letter written from Pembroke to Wharton, later than the one previously quoted, in late November, 1747.

> ....your mention of Mr Vane[29], reminds me of poor Smart (not that I, or any other mortal, pity him) about three weeks ago he was arrested here at the suit of a Taylor in London for a debt of about 50£ of three years standing. the College had about 28£ due to him in their Hands, the rest (to hinder him from going to the Castle , for he could not raise a shilling) Brown, May, & Peele, lent him upon his Note. upon this he remain'd confined to his room, lest his Creditors here should snap him; & the Fellows went round to make out a List of his debts, wch amount in Cambridge to above 350£. that they might come the readier to some Composition, he was advised to go off in the night, & lie hid somewhere or other. he has done so, & this has made the Creditors agree to an Aſsignment of 50£ per ann: out of his Income, wch is above 140£, if he lives at Cambridge (not else). but I am apprehensive, if this come to the Ears of Mr Vane he

[29] Henry Vane (1705-58), eldest son of Gilbert Vane, later Earl of Darlington (1754). Smart had an allowance of £40 a year made to him by the Duchess of Cleveland, and continued to him by the Duke, Vane's brother-in-law.

> may take away the 40£ hitherto allowed him by the Duke of Cleveland; for before all this (last Summer) I know they talked of doing so, as Mr Smart (they said) was settled in the World. if you found an Opportunity, poſsibly you might hinder this (wch would totally ruin him now) by representing his Absurdity in the best light it will bear: but at the same time they should make this a Condition of its Continuance; that he live in the College, soberly & within Bounds, for that upon any information to the Contrary it shall be absolutely stop'd. this would be doing him a real Service, tho' against the Grain: yet I must own, if you heard all his Lies, Impertinence, & Ingratitude in this affair, it would perhaps set you against him, as it has his only Friend (Mr Addison[30]) totally. & yet one would try to save him, for Drunkenneſs is one great Source of all this, & he may change it. I would not tell this matter in the North, were I you, till I found out it was known by other Means.

Smart's poetry is in many ways more acceptable to modern tastes than Gray's. Indeed, the editors of *Eighteenth Century Poetry*, David Fairer and Christine Gerrard, call Smart 'the most original voice in eighteenth-century poetry'. Lytton Sells, who curiously (since he was engaged in a biography of Gray) regarded Smart as the greater poet by far - 'one of the great ornaments of Cambridge' – and saw Gray as curmudgeonly, petty, and unpleasantly mean. Gray's attitude to Christopher Smart, like his attitude to the Jacobite trials, remains problematic. By the time of Smart's madness in 1759 his attitude had softened and he wrote to Mason of 'poor Smart' and was persuaded to give a

[30] Smart's old tutor, Leonard Addison (1699-1772), Fellow of Pembroke 1722.

guinea for Garrick's benefit production.

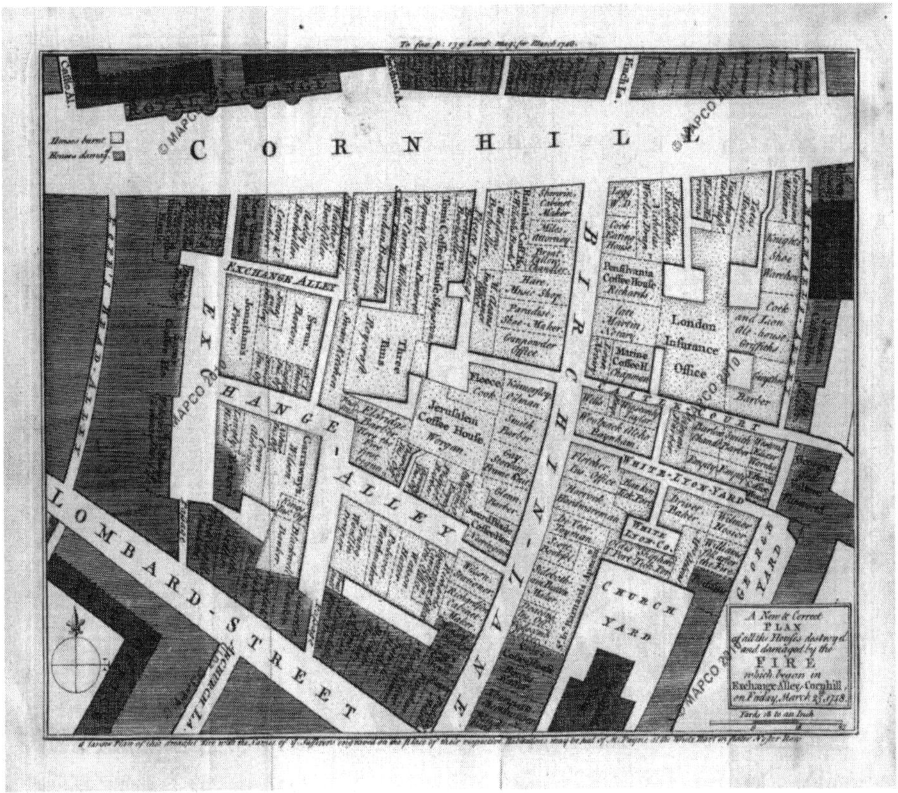

The fire in Cornhill 1748: the central area, un-shaded, was all burnt. Gray's house is shown top right in Cornhill, as occupied at that time by a Mrs Sarrazin, milliner.

From The London Magazine, 1748, p.139
(Public Domain)

Chapter Ten

1748 March: fire in Cornhill.
Until April: Cambridge.
April to November: London, Stoke, Strawberry Hill.
November: Cambridge.

Gray's letters rarely mention the mundane matters of household expenses, legal matters, or other logistical details. But in 1748 he had a problem with one of his properties in Cornhill: the destruction by fire of the house where he had been born. For this he needed the advice and ultimately the help (by way of a loan) of his good friend, Dr Wharton. In June he wrote from Stoke the following letter.

> Tho' I have been silent so long; do not imagine, I am at all leſs sensible to your Kindneſs, w^{ch} (to say the Truth) is of a Sort, that however obvious & natural it may seem, has never once occurr'd to any of my good Friends in Town, where I have been these seven Weeks. their Methods of Consolation were indeed very extraordinary: they were all sorry for my Loſs, that I could not chuse but laugh. one offer'd me Opera-Tickets, insisted on carrying me to the Grand-Masquereade, desir'd me to sit for my Picture. others asked me to their Concerts, or Dinners & Suppers at their Houses; or hoped, I would drink Chocolate with them, while I stayed in Town. all my Gratitude (or, if you please, my Revenge) was to accept of every thing they offer'd me: if it had been but a Shilling, I would have taken it. thank Heaven I was in good Spirits; else I could not have done it. I profited all I was able of their Civilities, & am returned into the Country loaded with their Bontés & Politeſses, but richer still in my own

> reflexions, wch I owe in great Measure to them too. ....Your Friendship has interested itself in my Affairs so naturally, that I cannot help troubling you with a little Detail of them. the House I lost was insured for 500£, & with the Deduction of 3 per C^{t} they paid me 485£, with wch I bought, when Stocks were lower, 525£. The rebuilding will cost 590, & other Expenses, that neceſsarily attend it, will mount that Summ to 650. I have an Aunt that gives me 100£; and another, that I hope will lend me what I shall want: but if (contrary to my Expectation) I should be forced to have recourse to your Aſsistance: it cannot be for above 50£; & that, about Xmas next when the Thing is to be finished. and now, my dear Wharton, why must I tell you a Thing so contrary to my own Wishes, & to yours, I believe? it is impoſsible for me to see you in the North, or to enjoy any of those agreeable Hours I had flatter'd myself with. I must be in Town several Times dureing the Summer; in August particularly, when half the Money is to be paid: the Relation, that used to do Things for me, is from Illneſs now quite incapable; & the good people here would think me the most careleſs & ruinous of Mortals, if I should think of such a Journey at this Time. the only Satisfaction I can pretend to, is that of hearing from you; & particularly about this Time, I was bid to expect good News[31].

The 'Loss' that this letter is mainly concerned with is the destruction by fire of the house in Cornhill where Gray was born. This happened as part of a more general and serious fire, an account of which appeared in *The Gentleman's Magazine* for 1748 (vol. xviii, p.138). 'Friday March 25. About 1 in the morning, a fire broke out at Mr Eldridge's (who with his wife, two daughters,

[31] The good news would be of the arrival of another baby in the Wharton family.

and a journeyman were burnt, and his lodger Mr *Cook*, kill'd by jumping out of a window) a peruke-maker in Exchange Alley, Cornhill; which burnt with great fury for 10 hours, and consumed almost all the houses in the said alley, and *Birchin Lane*, with the stately row of buildings in *Cornhill*, from *Change Alley* to *St Michael's Alley*, among which were several noted coffee-houses and taverns, five booksellers and many other valuable shops in Cornhill. Some accounts make the number of houses destroyed 160, but by the plan just published it appears to be no more than 80, and 14 or 15 damaged'.

Also interesting and relevant is an account of Gray's transactions with the insurance company after the fire, given in *The Correspondence of Thomas Gray* (*op cit.*, Vol. 1, p.305), and quoted from Bernard Drew's *The London Assurance; a Chronicle* (1928).

'When the devastating fire on March 25th, 1748, broke out in Cornhill and the lanes and alleys adjacent we learn from The London Magazine for the period in question that "no publick Office has been burnt except The London Assurance who had time to save their effects and have suffered only in the loss of their house". The Corporation, however, had an interest in another building not a stone's throw from their own. This was No. 41 Cornhill, the birthplace in 1716 of the poet Thomas Gray....The house was insured with the London Assurance for £500 and an entry in the Corporation's cash book exactly three weeks after the fire in Cornhill records the payment of £485 to Dorothy Gray (the poet's mother) in settlement of the claim. When we consider that the fire occurred on March 25th, and the cheque was signed by April 14th, we get some idea of the promptitude of the London Assurance in meeting its liabilities.... It may appear curious at first sight that Mrs Gray was only paid £485 on a £500 policy, but it is possible that the premises were not totally destroyed, or, on the other hand, that a 3% reduction was made for a speedy settlement....We know from Gray's letters that the house destroyed cost £650 to re-build, from which it would appear that Mrs Gray was considerably under-insured. The tenant at this time appears to have been one Sarrazine, a milliner....Today [i.e. 1928] the building is No. 39 Cornhill, and is occupied by the Union Discount Co. of London, while a tablet on the wall records the fact that Gray was born in a house which once stood upon that site."

Early in 1748 Dodsley published the first three volumes of his useful miscellany, called *A Collection of Poems*, for the plan of which he claimed an originality that it scarcely deserved, since, like the earlier miscellanies of Gildon and Tonson, it merely aimed at embracing in one work the best scattered poetry of the day. In the second volume were printed, without the author's name, three of Gray's odes - those *To Spring*, *On Mr Walpole's Cat*, and the *Eton Ode*.

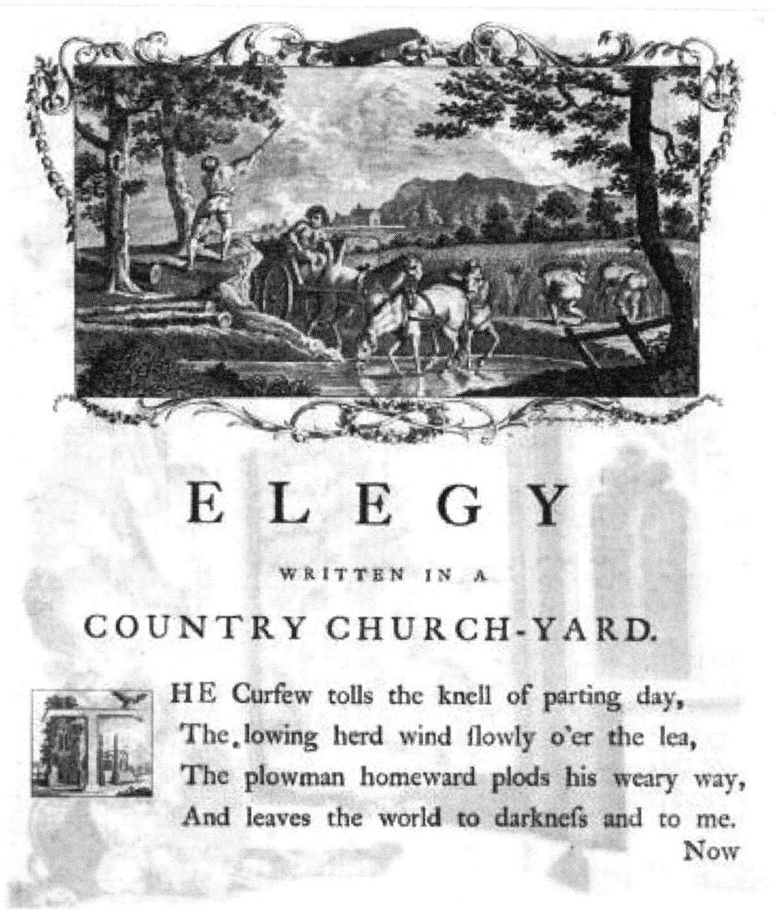

E L E G Y

WRITTEN IN A

COUNTRY CHURCH-YARD.

THE Curfew tolls the knell of parting day,
The lowing herd wind ſlowly o'er the lea,
The plowman homeward plods his weary way,
And leaves the world to darkneſs and to me.

Now

First Page of Dodsley's Quarto of *The Elegy*

CHAPTER ELEVEN

1751 Previous December to March: Cambridge
February: Publication of the ***Elegy***
March: Cambridge and London
March to June: Cambridge
June to September: Stoke and London
September to April of following year: Cambridge.

This is the year of the publication of *The Elegy*. Like many eighteenth-century poems, it circulated among an aristocracy of readers in manuscript first. It was forced into the public domain by the threat of a pirated version. Gray raised the alarm himself when he was contacted by the *Magazine of Magazines,*[32] who wished to publish the poem with his authority. It was actually published four days after Gray wrote to Walpole the following letter, on 15th February, 1751.

> My dear S^{r}, As you have brought me into a little Sort of Distreſs, you must aſsist me, I believe, to get out of it, as well as I can. yesterday I had the Misfortune of receiving a Letter from certain gentlemen (as their Bookseller expreſses it) who have taken the *Magazine of Magazines* into their hands. they tell me, that an ingenious Poem, call'd *Reflections in* a Country-Churchyard, has been communicated to them, wch they are printing forthwith: that they are inform'd, that the excellent Author of it is I by name, & that they beg not only his *Indulgence,* but the *Honour* of his Correspondence, &c. as I am not at all disposed to be either so indulgent or so correspondent as they desire; I have but one bad Way left to escape the Honour they would inflict upon me. & therefore am obliged to desire you would make Dodsley print it immediately (wch may be done in leſs than a week's time) from your Copy, but without my Name, in what Form is most

---

[32] *The Magazine of Magazines*, which was published for the best part of two decades, from 1751 to 1769, was a miscellany comprising extracts from numerous eighteenth-century periodicals and journals.

> convenient for him, but in his best Paper & Character. he must correct the Preſs himself, & print it without any Interval between the Stanzas, because the Sense is in some Places continued beyond them; & the Title must be, Elegy, wrote in a Country Churchyard. if he would add a Line or two to say it came into his Hands byAccident, I should like it better. if you think fit, the 102d Line may be read
>
> Awake, & faithful to her wonted Fires.
>
> but if this be worse than before; it must go, as it was. in the 126th, for *ancient* Thorn, read *aged.*
>
> If you behold the Mag: of Mag:s in the Light that I do, you will not refuse to give yourself this Trouble on my Account, wch you have taken of your own accord before now. Adieu, Sr, I am Yours ever TG:
> If Dodsley don't do this immediately, he may as well let it alone.

If the publication date of the Elegy is thus easily established, this is not the case with the date of its composition. Nobody really knows, but the likelihood is that it was first written in 1746. Gray speaks in an earlier letter, written in June in the previous year (1750), of 'a thing whose beginning you have seen long ago'. This was almost certainly *The Elegy*. But 'long ago' could mean 1742, as some protagonists argue, as well as 1746. The full context is as follows.

> I have been here at Stoke a few days (where I shall continue good part of the summer); and having put an end to a thing, whose beginning you have seen long ago, I immediately send it to you. You will, I hope, look upon it in the light of a thing with an end to it; a merit that most of my writings have wanted, and are like to want, but which this epistle I am determined shall not

want.....

The argument for 1742 as the date of composition is basically that this was a known period of literary activity for Gray and that this argument had the support of William Mason, Gray's close friend and later editor (who,however, did not meet Gray until 1747). Walpole had originally suggested that the poem had been started about four years after West's death, that is, in about 1746, but he later acceded to Mason's judgement, probably for the sake of a quiet life. Roger Lonsdale's verdict is that 'the most likely period for G. to have shown Walpole the beginning of the poem is in the autumn of 1746, when Walpole was living at Windsor and when G. saw him regularly'. Theories based upon speculations about whose death Gray may have been reacting to are not helpful.

What is clear is that the poem had a long period of gestation and that its end presented problems that required re-writing. The major problem is in the ending, which in one manuscript, the Eton MS, is quite different. The Eton MS ends with the following four stanzas:

The thoughtless World to Majesty may bow
Exalt the brave & idolise Success
But more to Innocence their Safety owe
Than power and genius e'er conspired to bless

And thou who mindful of the unhonour'd Dead
Dost in these Notes thy artless Tale relate
By Night and lonely Contemplation led
To linger in the gloomy Walks of Fate

Hark how the sacred Calm that broods around
Bids ev'ry fierce tumultuous Passion cease
In still small Accents whispering from the Ground
A grateful Earnest of eternal peace

No more with Reason and thyself at strife;
Give anxious Cares & endless Wishes room
But thro' the cool sequester'd Vale of Life
Pursue the silent tenour of they Doom.

When I write a poem, and then change it, my wife always prefers the first version. So here, Mason preferred this ending. Gray however, was discontented with it: 'a simple identification with the innocent but uneducated villagers', Lonsdale calls it. Instead, Gray substituted the enigmatic vision of the melancholy poet's death and his epitaph – 'melancholy marked him for her own' – an ending with much in common with the ending of *The Bard*: a vision of a heroic figure ultimately defeated by life.

The success of the poem was overwhelming and immediate. By 1763 twelve editions based on Dodsley's quarto had appeared. Since that time it has never been out of print, with countless editions, pirated versions, translations into different languages, and parodies. At one time every school-child learnt it by heart; now its popularity has waned and it is time for a revival. One of the best indices of its status as a national poem, however, is the story of General Wolfe's reference to it before the battle of Quebec in 1756, seemingly apocryphal but well-based in reliable evidence[33]. Wolfe is alleged to have said, as he drifted in a boat down the St Lawrence towards the Heights of Abraham and his surprise attack: 'I would rather have been the author of that piece than beat the French tomorrow'. Wolfe, being the man that he was - a cultured and intelligent man as well as a national hero - is the best of critics.

At first there was no criticism, only unbounded praise, but in recent times fault has been found with the underlying philosophy of the poem. Chief among the critics was William Empson. Empson criticized the anti-humanist ideas of the poem, its assumption that some are pre-destined to prosper, others to suffer, as if this social arrangement were part of the natural order of things. Persuasive and interesting as these remarks are, Lonsdale (who is surely the best judge, as Gray's detailed and most thorough editor) rejects them as 'irrelevant and misleading', on the grounds that they neglect the fact that the poet wishes to share the obscure destiny of the villagers, is personally involved with them, and rejects the attractions of the great world outside. The success of the poem is due to its honesty in facing up to 'the vast negative absolute of death'.... 'unable to refer it to a religious belief by which it can be made comprehensible'[34] .

Two small minor points seem worth making: first, that it is almost incredible that Gray never made a penny out of this poem, from a gentlemanly

---

[33] See F.G.Stokes, edition of the *Elegy*, Oxford, 1929.

[34] Wallace Jackson, *Thomas Gray*, The Poetry Foundation, Chicago, 2016)).

notion that it would be bad taste to do so; and second, that his instruction that the lines should be printed as a continuum ('print it without any Interval between the Stanzas, because the Sense is in some Places continued beyond them') is rarely if ever followed. It does make a difference to the feel and impact of the poem.

A View of Warwick Castle
Print by John Ryland 1763-1773

CHAPTER TWELVE

1752	April: London
	April to June: Cambridge
	June to October: Stoke with visits to Strawberry Hill and London
	October to following February: Cambridge.
1753	February to April: Stoke
	April to July: Cambridge
	July to October: Trip to the north
	October to December: Stoke and London
1754	January: Cambridge
	January to February: London
	February to June: Cambridge
	June to September: Stoke (T**our to Warwick**) and London.
	September to December: Cambridge.

In the fifties Gray carried out a number of explorations of midland England. In 1753 it was Northamptonshire that received most of his attention. It had been good weather. 'Never almost was such a year known for fruit. the Nectarines and best Peaches had been all gather'd three weeks before. the Grapes were then perfectly ripe, & still continue the best I ever eat in England.' Gray particularly had an eye for trees: 'the Hazle & Whitehorn were turning yellow in the hedges, the Sycamore, Lime, & Ash, & other Timber shew'd no signs of winter'. On a similar trip, a year later, it was historical reminders and antiquarian features that he noted. Walpole remarked that Gray was 'in flower' in these years. He wrote to Wharton from Stoke when he got back from Warwick in mid-September, 1754.

> I was in Northamptonshire, when I received your letter, but am now returned hither. I have been at **Warwick**, wch is a place worth seeing. the Town is on an eminence surrounded every way with a fine cultivated Valley, thro' wch the Avon winds, & at the distance of 5 or 6 miles, a circle of hills well wooded, & with various objects crowning them, that close the Prospect. out of the town on one side of it rises a rock, that might remind one of your rocks at Durham, but that it is not so savage, or so lofty, &

that the river, wch washes its foot, is perfectly clear, & so gentle, that its current is hardly visible. upon it stands the Castle, the noble old residence of the Beauchamps & Neville's, & now of Earl Brooke. he has sash'd the great Appartment, that's to be sure, (I can't help these things) & being since told, that square windows were not Gothic, he has put certain whim-whams withinside the glaſs, wch appearing through are to look like fretwork. then he has scooped out a little Burrough in the massy walls of the place for his little self & his children, wch is hung with Paper & printed Linnen, & carved chimney-pieces, in the exact manner of Berkley-square or Argyle-Buildings. what in short can a Lord do now a days that is lost in a great old solitary Castle, but sculk about, & get into the first hole he finds, as a Rat would do in like case. a pretty long old stone-bridge leads you into the town with a Mill at the end of it, over wch the rock rises with the Castle upon it with all its battlements & queer ruin'd towers, & on your left hand the Avon strays thro' the Park, whose ancient Elms seem to remember Sr Philip Sidney, (who often walk'd under them) and talk of him to this day. the Beauchamp Earls of Warwick lie under stately Monuments in the Choir of the great Church, & in our Lady's Chappel adjoining to it. there also lie Ambrose Dudley, E: of Warwick; & his Brother, the famous Ld. Leicester, with Lettice, his Counteſs. this Chappel is preserved entire, tho' the Body of the Church was burnt down 60 years ago, & rebuilt by Sr. C: Wren. I had heard often of Guy-Cliff two miles from the town, so I walked to see it, & of all improvers commend me to Mr Greathead, its present Owner. he shew'd it me himself, & is literally a fat young Man with a head & face much bigger than they are usually worn. it was naturally a very agreeable rock, whose Cliffs cover'd with large trees hung beetling over the Avon, wch twists twenty ways in sight of it. there was the Cell of Guy, Earl of Warwick, cut in the living stone, where he died a Hermit (as you may see in a penny

History, that hangs upon the rails in Moorfields). there were his fountains bubbling out of the Cliff; there was a Chantry founded to his memory in Henry the 6th's time. but behold the Trees are cut down to make room for flowering shrubs, the rock is cut up, till it is as smooth & as sleek as sattin; the river has a gravel-walk by its side; the Cell is a Grotta with cockle-shells and looking-glaſs; the fountains have an iron-gate before them, and the Chantry is a Barn, or a little House. even the poorest bits of nature, that remain, are daily threatened, for he says (& I am sure when the Greatheads are once set upon a thing, they will do it) he is determined, it shall be *all new*. These were his words, & they are Fate. I have been at Stow, at Woburn (the Duke of Bedford's), and at Wroxton (Ld Guilford's) but I defer these Chapters till we meet. I shall only tell you for your comfort, that the part of Northampt:^{re}, where I have been, is in fruits, in flowers, [& in] corn very near a fortnight behind this part of Buckinghamshire, that they have no nightingales, & that the other birds are almost as silent, as at Durham. it is rich land, but upon a Clay, & in a very bleak, high, exposed situation. I hope you have had some warm weather, since you last complained of the South. I have thoughts of seeing you about Michaelmas, tho' I shall not stay long in town. I should have been at Camb: before now, if the D: of Newc:^{le} & his foundation stone would have let me, but I want them to have done before I go. I am sorry Mr Brown should be the only one, that has stood upon Punctilio's with me, & would not write first. pray tell him so. Mason is (I believe) in town, or at Chiswick. [no news of Tuthill]: I wrote a long letter to him in answer to one he wrote me, but no reply. Adieu, I am ever Yrs. T G:

Gray was in satirical mood when he wrote to Wharton this report on his visit to Warwick. Sash windows were an eighteenth-century innovation and out of place in a medieval castle; hence the 'whimwhams'[35] – presumably mock-Gothic inserts – to disguise the modernity. Inside, of course, all was in the latest and most expensive taste. Pure linen wallpaper would be popular now, were it not so expensive (at £200 a roll from Laura Ashley). Berkley Square, now better known for the nightingales that he missed in Northamptonshire, might still be used as an epitome of a classy place in which to live; Argyle Buildings, off Oxford Street, are less well known but were being built in the 1740's for the upper ranks of society. Not only did the Duke of Argyle himself live there but also Lord Lyttleton, Sir Charles Wyndham, and Doctor Johnson's friend, Mrs Thrale. Gray kept the sharpest of his scorn, however, for Mr Greathead, who was then developing Guy's Cliff, a few miles from Warwick, with all the latest fashionable features: a grotto lined with cockle shells, a gravel walk, and a hermit's cave, authenticated by a penny ballad sheet.[36] The house that Greathead developed did not last long and eventually underwent many changes, from hospital in World War One to Boy's Home in World War Two to a ghost-haunting venue now: 'Warwickshire's hidden gem'. The serious item, however, in this letter is the item in brackets at the end: '[no news of Tuthill]'. Henry Tuthill was a close friend of Gray, admitted to Pembroke as a Cosin Scholar in 1740, graduating B.A. in 1743. In 1744 he was appointed Curate at Alconbury in Huntingdonshire and Gray's friend Wharton wanted him to be elected to a Fellowship at Pembroke, which eventually transpired. In 1757, however, out of the blue, Tuthill's fellowship was declared vacant, with a note in the College Register to the effect that Mr Tuthill had been 'guilty of great enormities'. One would guess that that could only mean one thing, confirmed perhaps by another mysterious note, this time in Mitford, that 'the name of Gray's friend, who drowned himself, was Tuthill'. The eighteenth-century had some curious attitudes to male association, tolerating men walking arm in arm (*vide* Admiral Croft and Colonel

---

[35] 'whim-wham'; something fanciful, a trifle' (OED)

[36] Moorfields was known as the place where ballad-mongers hung their wares, on the railings round the Bethlehem (or Bedlam) asylum.

Wallis in *Persuasion*) and yet coming down heavily on homosexual behaviour: anyone convicted of sodomy stood no chance of escaping the gallows. Gray could have been understandably worried about any taint or suggestion of homosexuality.

South-East View of Netley Abbey, William Bellers

Chapter Thirteen

1755 December to April: Cambridge
April to July: London, Stoke.
July: **The Vyne, trip to Portsmouth, Southampton, &c.**
August to November: Stoke, with visit to Strawberry Hill and London
November onwards: Cambridge.

In the first months of 1755 Gray appears to have been busy, first with *The Ode on the Progress of Poesy* and then with *The Bard*. The first of these poems, despite Robert Mack's extravagant praise of it, does very little for me and I understand, I think, why Gray had doubts about the poem's acceptability. *The Bard* is another matter. This is a brilliant poem, illustrated later by an equally brilliant painting by the northern artist, John Martin. The two belong together in their passion and their drama and have something important to say about the domination of the English and the crushing effect on Celtic culture. *The Bard* took two years to finish and owed its completion apparently to the emotional effect on Gray of a concert given in Cambridge by the blind harpist, John Parry, in May 1757.

In the summer Gray put the poem on one side and went down to The Vyne in Hampshire to visit his friend Chute. After a stay of a few days he went on to do a tour of the south coast and later described his journey in a letter to Wharton, written from Cambridge after his return in August 1755,.

> I wished for you often on the **Southern Coast**, where I have been, & made much the same Tour, that Stonehewer did before me. take notice, that the Oaks grow quite down to the Beach, & that the Sea forms a number of Bays little & great, that appear glittering in the midst of thick groves of them. add to this the Fleet (for I was at Portsmouth two days before it sail'd) & the number of Veſsels always passing along, or sailing up Southampton-River (w[ch] is the largest of these Bays I mention) and enters about 10 mile into the Land, & you will have a faint Idea of the South. from Fareham to Southampton, where you are

upon a level with the coast, you have a thousand such Peeps & delightful Openings, but would you see the whole at once, you must get upon Ports-Down 5 Mile on this side Portsmouth. it is the top of a ridge, that forms a natural Terraſs 3 Mile long, literally not three times broader than Windsor Terraſs with a gradual fall on both sides & cover'd with a turf like New-Market. to the North opens Hampshire & Berkshire cover'd with woods & interspersed with numerous Gentlemen's Houses & Villages. to the south, Portsmouth, Gosport, & c. just at your foot in appearance, the Fleet, the Sea winding, & breaking in bays into the land, the deep shade of tall Oaks in the enclosures, wch become blue, as they go off to distance, Portchester-Castle, Carshot-Castle, & all the Isle of Wight, in wch you plainly distinguish the fields, hedge-rows, & woods next the shore, & and a background of hills behind them. I have been also at Tichfield, at Netley-Abbey, (a most beautiful Ruin in as beautiful a situation) at Southampton, at Bevis-Mount, at Winchester, &c: my Gout is gone, but I am not absolutely well yet.

Richard Stonehewer had been with Gray in his midland travels in 1753. Elected to a fellowship at Pembroke in 1751, he was a good friend to Gray, practical, sensible, and seemingly good company. He must have given Gray the idea for this trip down to the south coast. Gray was in luck in seeing the fleet from Ports Down and it must indeed have been an impressive sight. In July a fleet of about 30 ships was mustered at Spithead and despatched under Admiral Boscawen to Canada in response to fears of French rivalry in that part of the world, a rivalry which broke out a year or so later in the Seven Years War. Unbeknownst to Gray, the fleet included a young ship's mate called James Cook. Gray showed some enterprise in searching out interesting places to visit. Bevis Mount was sited in the grounds of a country house called Padwell on the banks of the Itchen and was originally a vast pile of earth accumulated for defensive reasons in Saxon times. Tichfield was the site of a ruined abbey, where much of the building had been deliberately demolished to create a romantic ruin.

Horace Walpole followed Gray a month or so later, in September, and described his reactions in typically enthusiastic terms in a letter to Richard Bentley.

> The ruins are vast, and contain fragments of beautiful fretted roofs, pendant in the air, with all variety of Gothic patterns of windows, topped round and round with ivy. Many trees have sprouted up among the walls, and only want to be increased by cypreſses. A hill rises above the abbey, enriched with wood. The fort, in which we would build a tower for habitation[37], remains, with two small platforms. This little castle is buried from the abbey in wood, in the very centre, on the edge of a hill. On each side breaks in a view of the Southampton sea, deep blue, glistening with silver and veſsels; one side terminated by Southampton, on the other by Calshot Castle; and the Isle of Wight rises above the opposite hills. In short, they are not the ruins of Netley, but of Paradise. Oh, the purpled abbots! What a spot they had chosen to slumber in! The scene is so beautifully tranquil, yet so lively, that they seem only to have retired into the world.

Netley Abbey was already a pilgrimage site and was to attract Gray on a future visit, when he described it in more detail in a letter to James Brown, dated October 1764.

> I received your letter, before I left London, & sit down to write to you after the finest walk in the finest day, that ever shone, to Netley Abbey, my old friend, with whom I long'd to renew my acquaintance. my Ferryman (for one pasſes over a little arm of the sea about ½ a mile) asſured me, he would not go near it in

[37] Walpole suggested to the owner that he built a castle tower for habitation in one corner of the ruins.

> the night-time for all the world, tho' he knew much money had been found there. The sun was *all too glaring & too full of gauds*[38] for such a scene, wch ought to be visited only in the dusk of an evening. it stands in a little quiet valley, wch gradually rises behind the ruin into a half-circle crown'd with thick wood. before it on a descent is a thicket of oaks, that serves to veil it from the broad day & from profane eyes, only leaving a peep on both sides, where the sea appears glittering thro' the shade, & veſsels with their white sails, that glide across & are lost again. concealed behind the thicket stands a little Castle (also in ruins) immediately on the shore, that commands a view over an expanse of sea clear & smooth as glass (when I saw it) with Southampton & several villages 3 miles off to the right, Calshot-Castle at 7 miles distance, & the high lands of the Isle of Wight to the left, & in front the deep shades of the new Forest distinctly seen, because the water is no more than three miles over. the Abbey was never very large. the shell of its church is almost entire, but the pillars of the iles are gone, & the roof has tumbled in, yet some little of it is left in the transept, where the ivy has forced its way through, & hangs flaunting down among the fretted ornaments & escutcheons of the Benefactors. much of the lodgings & offices are also standing, but all is overgrown with trees & bushes, & mantled here & there with ivy, that mounts over the battlements.

As with many of Gray's travel objectives, Netley became a pilgrimage site for later Romantics. John Constable visited Netley in 1816 and drew a study of the East Window of the abbey [V.& A. 823-1888]. He later submitted a painting of the abbey by moonlight as an illustration to stanza V for inclusion in an edition of Gray's *Elegy* [British Museum, Watercolour, 1833]. Turner too visited the area with his sketchbook, though it is not clear if this was as early as 1795 or as late as 1832. Other Romantic painters were similarly fascinated by

---

[38] A slight mis-quotation from Shakespeare's *King John*, Act 3, scene 3.

the combination of ghostly aspect and age and ruin. They may not have been directly following Gray's example but this following of Gray's example, what we may call the Gray Effect, was probably due to the publication in the 1780's of *A Supplement to the Tour (*also later published under the title, *The Travellers' Companion)* by George Kearsley (see also p. 84). This was an apparently pirated version of Gray's personal atlas, on which he had kept notes on the places he had visited or wanted to visit[39]. The British Library now has the original, the verso of the map on Hampshire duly bearing a note about 'Netley Abbey, E.S.E. of Southampton', and carrying an asterisk for special attention. The Library has other copies belonging to various unknown gentlemen, who made their own notes, making it clear that the influence of the book was widespread.

[39] Kearsley's Introduction states, 'This catalogue was originally written on the blank pages of Kitchen's *English Atlas* by Mr Gray. His own extensive researches into the topography of this island furnished him with many of the particulars; the summer tours which he made supplied him with more; and to these he was frequently adding from the information of such persons on whose taste and judgement he could best depend.'

View of Pembroke Hall, engraving after Joshua Baldry, 1807,
From the Cambridge University Almanac

CHAPTER FOURTEEN

1756 Previous November to April: Cambridge
March: **Move from Peterhouse to Pembroke**
April: London
April to June: Cambridge
June to December: London and Stoke
December: Back to Cambridge

March 1756 saw a major disruption in Gray's life. An undergraduate trick was played upon him, which resulted in his moving from Peterhouse across the road to Pembroke. Mason [*Memoirs*, p.241] gives the following short account of what happened.

> 'Two or three young Men of Fortune, who lived in the same staircase, had for some time intentionally disturbed him with their riots, and carried their ill behaviour so far as frequently to awaken him at midnight. After having borne with their insults longer than might reasonably have been expected from a man of less warmth of temper, Mr Gray complained to the Governing part of the society; and not thinking his remonstrance was sufficiently attended to, quitted the College. The slight manner in which he mentions this affair, when writing to his most intimate friends, certainly does honour to the placability of his disposition'.

Mason was doing his best to defend Gray against a charge of not having a sense of humour, trying to create an image of a sensible and reasonable man against any suspicion of his being an over-sensitive prissy old woman. Edmund Gosse gave a fuller account, without completely answering that charge.

> On the 9th January 1756 he (Gray) asked Dr Wharton to buy him a rope-ladder of a man in Wapping who advertised such

> articles[40]. It was to be rather more than thirty-six feet long, with strong hooks at the top. This machine Wharton promptly forwarded, and Gray proceeded to have an iron bar fixed within his bedroom window. This bar, crossing a window which looks towards Pembroke still exists and marks Gray's chambers at Peterhouse. Such preparations however, could not be made without attracting great attention in the latter college, where Gray was by no means a favourite among the high-coloured young gentlemen who went bull-baiting to Heddington or came home drunk and roaring from cock-shying at Market Hill. Accordingly the noisy fellow-commoners determined to have a lark at the timid little poet's expense, and one night in February 1756, when Gray was asleep in bed, they suddenly alarmed him with a cry of fire on his staircase, having previously placed a tub of water under his window. The ruse succeeded only too well: Gray, without staying to put on his clothes, hooked his rope-ladder to the iron-bar, and descended nimbly into the tub of water, from which he was rescued with shouts of laughter by the unmannerly youths

Gosse then attacks the prank by saying that 'to our modern ideas this outrage on a harmless middle-aged man of honourable position, who had done nothing whatever to provoke insult or injury, is almost inconceivable'. But the damage in Gosse's account had already been done in the description of Gray as 'the timid little poet'. There is a better defence, which is that Gray's fear of fire was entirely reasonable in an eighteenth-century context and his precaution against it was a wholly sensible one, which was indeed copied elsewhere. This reputation for timidity is not wholly deserved and does much harm to our appreciation of Gray as a man capable of considerable enterprise and originality.

Gray's own account of his side of the story is given in two letters to

---

[40] Before laughing at this contrivance, it is worth reflecting on the fact that it is still possible to buy rope ladders attached to bars bent so as to hang from an upstairs window as a sensible means of escape.

Wharton, one in January ordering the rope-ladder, and the second giving the account of the move.

> ....you who give yourself the trouble to think of my health, will not think me very troublesome if I beg you to bespeak me a Rope-Ladder (for my neighbours everyday make great progreſs in drunkenness, w[ch] gives me reason to look about me) it must be full 36 Foot long, or a little more, but as light & manageable as may be, easy to unroll, & not likely to entangle. I never saw one, but I suppose it must have strong hooks, o something equivalent, a-top, to throw over an iron-bar[41] to be fix'd withinside of my window. however you will chuse the proprest form, & instruct me in the use of it. I see an Ephraim Hadden near Hermitage Stairs[42] in Wapping that advertises them, but perhaps you may find a better Artisan near you. this with a Canister of Tea & another of Snuff, w[ch] I left at your house, & a Pound of Soap from Mr Field (for mine is not so good here) will fill a Box, w[ch] I beg the favour of you to send [me], when you can conveniently.
>
> My best compliments to M[rs] Wharton. I am ever Yours TG:

The second letter was dated March 25th and was written to Wharton from Pembroke, to give a toned down version of the events.

> Dear Doctor
>
> Tho' I had no reasonable excuse or myself before I received your last letter, yet since that time I have had a pretty good one, having been taken up in quarrelling with Peter-house, & removing myself to Pembroke. this may be look'd upon as a sort

[41] A bar, supposed to have been fixed for the purpose of supporting a rope-ladder, is still to be seen outside the window of Gray's rooms at Peterhouse.

[42] There is still a Hermitage Stairs by the river in Wapping.

of Æera in a life so barren of events as mine, yet I shall treat it in Voltaire's manner, & only tell you that I left my lodgings, because the rooms were noisy, & the People of the house dirty. this is all I would chuse to have said about it; but if you in private should be curious enough to enter into a particular detail of facts & minute circumstances, Stonhewer who was witneſs to them will probably satisfy you. all, I shall say more, is, that I am for the present extremely well lodged here, & as quiet as in the Grande Chartreuse; & that every body (even the Dr Longs & Dr Mays) are as civil, as they could be to Mary de Valence[43] in person....

[43] The foundress of Pembroke Hall

York Minster, South East View
Drawn and etched by J.C.Buckler, 1816.

CHAPTER FIFTEEN

1757	To March: Cambridge March to April: London April to June: Cambridge June to December: London and Stoke (& Strawberry Hill)
1758	Previous December to April: Cambridge. April to May: London May to June: Cambridge, with tour to Ely, Peterborough etc. June to July: London and Stoke, Hampton Court, & Strawberry Hill. July to December: Stoke, with brief visit to London in October.

William Palgrave was the son of a physician at Norwich. He took his degree at Pembroke, presumably meeting Gray in his time there, and was ordained deacon in 1759, later becoming rector of Thrandeston and Palgrave in Suffolk. Although he was twenty years younger than Gray, he became a trusted friend, sharing his antiquarian interests. As an index of Gray's confidence and closeness, he was distinguished by being addressed with one of Gray's not-very-complimentary nicknames, 'Old Pa', or 'Proud Palgrave' or 'The Abbé' (cf. 'Skroddles' for Mason, 'Dragon of Wantly's Dam' for Mrs Oliffe); it would also appear that Gray pronounced the name Palgrave, without the l ("pawgrave"). Palgrave had his uses for verifying details about old buildings or ancient family trees; his reward was being guided on his Grand Tour with notes from Gray on what he should particularly look out for.

The fragment of a letter to Palgrave included here is particularly interesting because of its provenance. It survives, by some miracle, as an item in an autograph collection. Collecting autographs was popular in the nineteenth century and one of the most adept at this dangerous pastime - dangerous because of its consequences for posterity - was a certain Lady Charnwood, wife of Godfrey Benson, first Lord Charnwood. Lady Charnwood was in a privileged position for this activity. Her husband was himself a writer and had a wide circle of literary friends, with frequent meetings and house-parties. Lady Charnwood could make an impressive collection of autographs from among her immediate acquaintances. But she did not stop there. Invalided by a carriage accident, she probably needed a pursuit that she could follow in the sedentary life to which she was confined. The results of her endeavours can be seen in four large folders in the British Library's manuscript collection, each containing hundreds of autograph documents. These are not snippets of signatures cut off the bottoms of letters but whole documents: a four-page letter from William Cowper to Lady Hesketh, a delightful two-page note from Jane Austen to her niece, and this fragment of a letter from Gray to William Palgrave.

> Dugdale[44] mentions (as if it still existed) a Chappel of the Virgin on the North-side of the Church; if this be true, it is the oldest part of the whole, being founded by A:^{p} Roger in Henry 2^{d}'s time. be sure to look for it.
>
> Can you distinguish in the S: Transept two different styles that of Richard 1st's time, & that of Henry 3^{d}'s? & in the rest of ye building three more kinds of architecture, that of Edw: 1st in the N: Transept; of Edw: 2^{d} in the Nave, & West-Front; & of Edw: 3^{d} in the Choir, & great Tower.
>
> Is there any difference in the building of ye Lady-Choir, & the ornaments bestow'd upon it?
>
> Pray, be particular in describing the parts of this Cathedral, w^{ch} (as I remember) is the great School of the Goths.
>
> There was a building of Edw: 4th's reign (call'd Sir William's College[45]) for the Chantry-Priests near this Church. where is it now, & what other old fragments remain of the cloisters, Palace, &c: go into the Vaults under the Choir, if you can.

---

[44] Sir William Dugdale (1605-86), antiquarian, author of *Monasticon Anglicanum*, 'a History of the abbeys, and other monasteries, hospitals, frieries & cathedral and collegiate churches'. Gray had his own copy of this author's *Baronage of England*, now in the Bodleian, heavily annotated.

[45] St William's College is named after William of York (died 1154) and is next to York Minster. It was established between 1465 and 1467 with the permission of King Edward IV as the home for chantry priests of the Cathedral. Not clear why Gray refers to 'Sir William'. It is now a venue for expensive weddings.

[*August 1758: conjectural date, since Palgrave was known (see letter 279) to be travelling in Yorkshire in the summer of 1758*.]

Lady Charnwood had experienced problems in obtaining a specimen of Thomas Gray's handwriting.: 'his letters are hardly ever on the market' (Charnwood, *An Autograph Collection*, London: Benn, 1930, p.47). She seems to have been quite aware of the biographical value of letters as 'an enlightenment as to their personality' but completely unaware of what damage she might be doing to future collections of letters. She defends herself against any criticism, however, by declaring that autograph letters are not 'showy' (and so not really valuable?) and speaks of herself as 'a humble amateur of slender means', adding that the Americans are the ones who are buying up all the valuable autographs. What certainly was going on, at a time when Gray's reputation was still enormously high, was that books, belonging to him, and especially those bearing his marginalia, were becoming highly collectable items. Gray was an active marginalist, writing in the margins of most of his books, in a way which my generation was strongly dissuaded from doing. The result is that the National Art Library, through the collections of Forster and Dyce[46], has a considerable number of Gray's books, some of them with the most interesting additions: cookery recipes, for example, or bird drawings, and detailed descriptions of insects. And Gray's marginalia is to be found, not only in the Victoria and Albert, but also in almost every learned library one would care to name. We get another view of Gray from these off-the-cuff observations on matters that one would not have realised engaged his attention so completely.

Gray appears to have been collecting notes of a topographical nature on all the places of antiquarian or scenic interest that he had visited, and also of a few that he hadn't yet planned. Word of his thoroughness in this regard must have circulated, for people came to him for guidance about places that they should see when doing a tour, either at home or in France or Italy. After Gray's death, his close friend Mason published the notes that Gray had made on the obverse side of the pages of his copy of *Ellis's Atlas of the British Isles* (see the copy in the British Library manuscript collection) and this in turn was copied

[46]. John Forster (1812-76) and Alexander Dyce (1798-1869), literary scholars and collectors and benefactors of the Victoria and Albert Museum)

by a less scrupulous printer (already mentioned on page 100). The result was a work with one of those typically long 18th century titles: *A Supplement to the Tour Through Great-Britain, containing a Catalogue of the antiquities, houses, parks, plantations, scenes, and situations, in England and Wales... By The Late Mr. Gray... To which are now added, by another Hand, Several Additions...* London: G. Kearsley, 1787.

Gray's questioning in the letter to Palgrave is very specific and searching. With no Pelican Guide to help him and the study of architectural history in an undeveloped state, he was struggling to detect and differentiate the changes visible in the 300 years of building manifested at York in a style for which he had a special interest, Gothic.[47] York is one of the great Gothic cathedrals of northern Europe, 'the great school of the Goths', in Gray's words. Gray presumably meant that this cathedral was to be considered the exemplar for this style of ecclesiastical architecture. Not until Rickman in 1817, however, were the terms Early English, Decorated, and Perpendicular available to describe the differences that Gray thought he saw in the transepts of York Minster. Indeed, Gray's divisions by royal reigns do roughly coincide with the terms now used (1100-1300 Early English/ *Richard II and Henry II*; 1300-1350 Decorated/ *Edward I*; 1350 -1400 Perpendicular/ *Edward II and Edward III*). It takes an expert eye, however, to see these changes demonstrated in the stylistic differences in the North and South Transepts. Most visitors now would be looking for the Five Sisters window in the North transept and the Rose Window in the South – and would not be able to tell that the South transept is slightly earlier than the North. Gray's historical way of looking at things is arguably better than the modern architectural method, in that it links us better to the dates[48]. Gray's historical knowledge would also tell him that

---

[47] 'Mr Gray's love of and knowledge in Gothic architecture are well known' – Norton Nicholls, *Reminiscences of Gray*, 1805, p.52.

[48] According to William Mason, Gray traced the development of English medieval architecture from its origins to the time of Elizabeth I, relying upon 'that internal evidence which the buildings themselves give of their respective antiquity', and in so doing, was 'enabled to pronounce, at first sight, on the precise time, when any particular part of any of our cathedrals was erected'. [Marion Roberts, Architectural History, Vol.36, 1993, *Thomas Gray's Contribution to the Study of Medieval Architecture*]

any trace of a Chapel of the Virgin would have been destroyed in the times of the Civil War or even earlier during the Reformation; no harm, however, in sending Palgrave to look for some sign of the old religion. Archbishop Roger de Pont l'Eveque whom Gray mentions as the founder of the cathedral was a colourful character, accused of homosexuality at one point, excommunicated by Becket at another. Gray's detailed knowledge of the background history of the places he visited was voluminous. He even expected the poor Palgrave to penetrate into the foundations of the cathedral, which would not then have been made safe and interesting, as they are now, with historical displays in the Undercroft – and surprisingly without a coffee shop.

Bedford Square, looking out on Bedford Gardens, drawn by T.H. Shepherd, 1808-64

CHAPTER SIXTEEN

1759 March to June: London.
June to July: Cambridge.
July: took up residence in London.
September: Stoke (Lady Cobham's)
October onwards: London (with visit to **Strawberry Hill**)

In July of this year, 1759, Gray decided on a major shift of residence, from Cambridge to London. By moving to a set of rooms in Southampton Row, he acquired for himself a view over gardens and away to the north to the villages of Highgate and Hampstead. He also moved to be closer to the newly opened British Museum. Pleased with the change, though with some guarded reservations, he wrote to William Palgrave in July, soon after the move.

> I am now settled in my new territories commanding Bedford Gardens, and all the fields as far as Highgate and Hampstead, with such a concourse of moving pictures as would astonish you; so *rus-in-urbe-ish*, that I believe I shall stay here, except little excursions and vagaries, for a year to come. What though I am separated from the fashionable world by broad St.Giles's, and many a dirty court and alley, yet here is air, and sunshine, and quiet, however, to comfort you: I shall confeſs that I am basking with heat all the summer, and I suppose I shall be blown down all the winter, besides being robbed every night; I trust, however, that the Museum, with all its manuscripts and rarities by the cart-load, will make ample amends for all the aforesaid inconveniencies.
>
> I this day past through the jaws of the great leviathan into the den of Dr Templeman, superintendent of the reading-room, who congratulated himself on the sight of so much good company. We were, first, a man that writes for Lord Royston; 2dly, a man that writes for Dr Burton , of York; 3dly, a man that writes for the Emperor of Germany, or Dr Pocock, for he speaks

the worst English I ever heard; 4thly, Dr Stukeley, who writes for himself, the very worst person he could write for; and lastly, I, who only read to know if there be anything worth writing, and that not without difficulty. I find that they printed 1000 copies of the *Harleian Catalogue*, and have only sold fourscore; that they have £900 a year income, and spend £1300, and are building apartments for the under-keepers; so I expect in winter to see the collection advertised and set to auction.

Have you read Lord Clarendon's Continuation of his History? Do you remember Mr --'s account of it before it came out? How well he recollected all the faults, and how utterly he forgot all the beauties. Surely the groſsest taste is better than such a sort of delicacy.

This seems to have been a busy year in Gray's life but the truth is that there were long stretches in his life in which he seems to have done little or nothing, in which his main problem was in battling against the depression that comes often with idleness. His main solution was to retreat into books. He acquired books like most bibliophiles without thought of where to put them all, and built up a formidable library, specializing on the classics, of course, and on travel books.[49] He read, apparently tirelessly and with extraordinary powers of concentration. He also made notes on his books - literally on them, in the margins, for no real purpose.

I was brought up to respect books and not to mark them in any way. This was not the way of the eighteenth-century when many books were printed with deliberately wide margins for the addition of notes. Gray certainly used his books to comment and amend, not in the manner of the modern student, whose pencil marks one so often finds in university library copies ("Rubbish!", "Ridiculous!", etc.). Gray's marginal notes in his copy of Clarendon, which must have been a favourite book, are thorough and detailed, correcting details of family history, making minute corrections in the account of the Rebellion,

---

[49] See W.P.Jones, *Thomas Gray Scholar*, Cambridge: Harvard U.P., 1937 for a list of the books in Gray's library (p.151).

which clearly fascinated him. For whom was he making these notes? Who was he addressing? Much of his life must have been of this nature, a silent conversation with himself, because there was no-one else who quite shared his interests and attitudes. Gray's marginalia can be found in a multitude of books. Curiously, Gray's personal copy of *Flora Anglia*, William Hudson's 1762 survey of British plants, made its uncharted way into the reserve collections of the Carlisle Library, with the assertion, "The notes in this book were wrote by the celebrated Mr Gray the poet". Not completely true, because some of the notes are in an unidentified hand, but Gray's unmistakable handwriting is certainly there, most obviously in a note in the fly: "To cure hams. Sal. Petr. 1.0 oz. Treacle coarsest sugar & salt, each ½ a pound. 3 cloves of garlic". The British Library owns another marginalia treasure, Gray's copy of *Verral's Cookery*. Gray has added detailed notes and a number of recipes.: for example, a recipe for "Veal stew'd with Rice. Boil the veal till it is enough with an onion in it; then take it out, and strain off the broth, put the rice into it & a little mace & let it stew, till it is done enough. Thicken it up with a little flower & butter. Put the veal into the rice to warm & serve it up. Half a pound of rice is sufficient for 4 pounds of veal'. With the reservations that Gray's quantities tend to be on the large side, these recipes work and must have been used. My wife experimented on the recipe for Oxford Pudding, a kind of summer pudding with currants, sugar, lemon, eggs, suet, bread, and the result was a very tasty 'afters'. Norman Nicholson has a curious 'take' on this interest of Gray's. 'We are reminded that, like many men who are deprived of normal sexual experience, Gray occasionally found a compensatory pleasure in good food and good cooking'. My own interpretation would be that it is an interest that makes him that bit more normal, rather than a bit less, more the kind of man who would enjoy tinkering in the kitchen and trying out the results. Gray also had his own copy of Linnaeus's *Systema Naturae* and his notes on the plants and birds described therein are particularly interesting. C.E.Norton made a study of this enterprise as long ago as 1903 but his conclusion is nevertheless particularly relevant. 'The work which these volumes exhibit is so remarkable a monument to Gray's learning and industry, and throws so much light on his occupations and interests, especially during the last ten years of his life, that some knowledge of it seems essential, not only to the understanding of the course of his days, but even more to a just appreciation of his character and his acquisitions'.

In all this note-taking, he was not researching a book, simply adding to his knowledge, his acquired learning[50]. And so the opening of the British Museum in Montague House was a godsend and Gray was one of its first customers/readers. The British Museum began when Sir Hans Sloane, the physician and naturalist, bequeathed his collection of 71,000 rarities to the nation in January 1753; to this were added the collections of Cotton and Harley and the old library of the Kings of England. It took six months to find a home for these objects and to select a committee to run the organization and to find a Reading room superintendent, Dr Templeman, and to issue a book of rules. The Museum opened to the public on 15th January, 1759, with free admission to 'all studious and curious Persons'. Gray certainly came into that category. He must have read Clarendon's History in the reading room but he eventually bought his own copy and this is now in the Bodleian Library in Oxford, complete with Gray's annotations in the margins.

It is difficult now to imagine, as one walks round Bedford Square, that at one time this would be at the edge of the city and one would be able to see across to Hampstead. One must be grateful that the eighteenth-century squares and their gardens have survived at all and kept this as such a pleasant part of London. Gray needed to be near the countryside to make his observations of wind and sky, bird and insect, plant and tree.

---

50 Possibly not true. LaRue Van Hook (*Classical Scholarship of Thomas Gray*, American Journal of Philology, 1936) declares that Gray had 'ambitious plans for the editing of Greek authors' but it is not clear where he can find evidence for this.

Strawberry Hill: The Holbein Chamber

CHAPTER SEVENTEEN

1759 February to March: Cambridge
March to June: London
June to July: Cambridge
July: took up residence in London.
September: Stoke (Lady Cobham's)
October onwards: London (with visit to **Strawberry Hill**)

The Strawberry Hill project occupied Horace Walpole for a number of years and Gray must have been privy to each new development. In May 1747 Horace Walpole took a lease on a small 17th-century house that was "little more than a cottage", with 5 acres (20,000 m^2) of land from a Mrs. Chenevix. The following year he purchased the house which the original owner, a coachman, had named "Chopped Straw Hall". Finding an old lease that described his land as "Strawberry Hill Shot", Walpole adopted this new name for his soon-to-be "elegant villa". In stages, Walpole rebuilt the house to his own specifications, giving it a Gothic style and expanding the property to 46 acres over the years. He had the advice of a small Committee of Taste, made up of himself, Richard Bentley, and John Chute. Walpole later made it clear who the major influence was. "[Chute] was my oracle in taste, the standard to whom I submitted my trifles, and the genius that presided over poor Strawberry!"[51] Gray was not a member of the Committee but he was frequently consulted and did frequently visit. So, the 'little plaything house', as it began, grew in independent style, size, and architectural aim. As Rosemary Hill notes, "Strawberry Hill was the first house without any existing medieval fabric to be [re-]built from scratch in the Gothic style and the first to be based on actual historic examples, rather than an extrapolation of the Gothic vocabulary first developed by William Kent. As such it has a claim to be the starting point of the Gothic Revival."[52] Gray wrote to Dr Wharton with the latest news on the project in September 1759, from his lodgings in London.

---

[51] Letter from Walpole to Mann, May 27, 1776.

[52] *"Welcome to Strawberry Hill*", TLS, 19 May, 2010.

> Mr. W: has lately made a new Bed-chamber, w[ch] as it is in the best tast of anything he has yet done, & in your own Gothic way, I must describe a little. you enter by a peaked door at one corner of the room (out of a narrow winding passage, you may be sure) into an Alcove, in which the bed is to stand, formed by a screen of pierced work opening by one large arch in the middle to the rest of the chamber, wch is lighted at the other end by a bow-window of three bays, whose tops are of rich painted glaſs in mosaic. the cieling is coved & fretted in star and quatrefoil compartments, with roses at the intersections, all in papier-maché. the chimney on your left is the high altar in the cathedral of Rouen (from whence the Screen also is taken) consisting of a low surbased Arch between two octagon Towers, whose pinnacles almost reach the Ceiling, all of Nich-work. the chairs & dreſsing-table are real carved ebony, pick'd up at auctions. the hangings uniform purple paper, hung all over with the Court of Henry, y[e] 8th, copied after the Holbein's in the Queen's Closet at Kensington, in black & gold frames. the bed is to be either from Burleigh (for L[d] Exeter is new-furnishing it, & means to sell some of his original household-stuff) of the rich old tarnish'd embroidery; or if that is not to be had, & it must be new, it is to be a cut velvet with a dark purple pattern on a stone-colour sattin-ground, & deep mixt fringes, & tassels. there's for you, but I want you to see it. in the mean time I live in the Musæum, & write volumes of antiquity.....

Gray had presumably recently returned from a visit to Strawberry Hill and was seemingly very impressed with the latest additions - 'in the best Tast of anything he has yet done'.His real attitude can perhaps be guessed from the non-commital 'There's for you' at the end: not so much non-commital, in fact, as distancing Gray from what he must have viewed as a spurious artistic experiment.

W. S Lewis gives a long list of the outstanding changes made in the 1758 building programme in his essay on the Genesis of Strawberry Hill[53]. Specifically of the Holbein room, he explains that, 'It was a bedroom lined with tracings of the Holbeins "taken off on oil-paper by Vertue from the original drawings of Holbein in Queen Caroline's closet at Kensington, now removed to Buckingham-house" and its ceiling was taken from the Queen's dressing room at Windsor. Walpole had seen a "Holbein room" at Cowdray nine years before. The chimney piece, designed by Bentley, was "chiefly" taken from the tomb of Archbishop Warham at Canterbury. A remarkable feature of the room was an ecclesiastical screen, the "pierced arches" of which were copied from the gates of the choir of Rouen; the rest of the screen was Bentley's.' Walpole's technique was not dissimilar to that employed by the Scottish ship-owner, William Burrell, in buying up parts of houses, statues, windows etc., and re-assembling them in mixed fashion in a house of his own creation [beautifully re-created now in the Burrell Collection at Pollock House, near Glasgow]. Lewis confirms this technique in a later comment from the same essay. "Strawberry Hill may be said to have been assembled rather than built, for Walpole's method was, briefly, to copy admired details of Gothic buildings (especially tombs) and translate them into whatever was required at the moment. He did this by going back to the buildings themselves or to prints of them, thus eliminating all question of the genuineness of his "Gothic."..... Strawberry was an assemblage of historic examples of Gothic art fitted into a Georgian frame." A second letter about Strawberry Hill, dated August 5th, 1763 and written from Cambridge, has some further comments at the end.

> You may well wonder at my long taciturnity: I wonder too, & know not what cause to a sign. For it is certain, I think of you daily. I believe it is owing to the nothingneſs of my history, for except six weeks that I pasſ'd in Town towards the end of spring, & a little jaunt to Epsom & Box Hill, I have been here time out of mind in a place, where no events grow, tho' we preserve those of former days by way of Hortus Siccus in our libraries. My

[53] W.S.Lewis, *The Genesis of Strawberry Hill*, Metropolitan Museum Studies, Vol. 5/No.1, pp.57-92, August 1934.

> slumbers were disturbed the other day by an unexpected visit from Mr. W: who dined with me, seem'd mighty happy for the time he stay'd & said he could like to live here: but hurried home in the evening to his new Gallery, wch is all Gothicism, & gold & crimson, & looking-glaſs. He has purchased at an auction in Suffolk ebony chairs & old moveables enough to load a wagon.

Eighteen ebony chairs and two tables cost all of £45 (£9,000 at today's values) at Lady Conyers's sale at Great Stoughton in Huntingdonshire (see note in the *Correspondence*, Vol.II, p. 805). 'Gothicism' here appears to be a term of praise; but it was not always so. The OED gives the primary meaning of the word as 'rudeness, barbarism' and elsewhere in the letters that is how the word is used. See page 38 for Gray's criticism of a painting by Raphael for its 'Gothicism'.

"Strawberry Hill Gothic" is, nevertheless, a commonly accepted term in the architectural phrase book, though the style is also sometimes referred to, mockingly, as 'Disneyland Gothic'. The question is whether Walpole created an authentic architectural style, or whether the whole thing can be dismissed as a caprice or 'playful mishmash'. Part of that debate depends upon the asymetry of the house. 'Walpole's was a sly mind', according to Peter Guillery[54], 'perfectly capable of harbouring and even delighting in inherently contradictory outlooks. From the first with Walpole at Strawberry Hill there is a tension between regularization and a fondness for irregularity'. While the rest of the nation was busy building imposing residences in a strictly regular classical style, Walpole had the confidence to strike out in his own fashion, aiming only, in surprisingly humble fashion, at 'a little Gothic Castle'.

Strawberry Hill had an influence on the design of domestic interiors and furniture. It also helped to give birth to the Gothic novel as a literary genre, a line which developed after the publication of *The Castle of Otranto* in 1764 and which includes Anne Radcliffe's *Mysteries of Udolpho* (1794) and Jane Austen's *Northanger Abbey* (1818). The relationship of Strawberry Hill to *The Castle of*

---

[54] Peter Guillery, *Strawberry Hill: Building and Site*, Architectural History Vol. 38, 1995, pp. 102-128.

Otranto is put succinctly by W.S.Lewis. “It is something more than a cliché of criticism to say that *The Castle of Otranto* and Strawberry Hill are one and the same ". Lewis proceeds to find a setting for many of the scenes in the novel in particular rooms at Strawberry Hill. “That Matilda's apartment is the Holbein Chamber seems certain from its position relative to "the postern gate," which is clearly the north entrance at Strawberry.” And Lewis sums up with a tribute to Walpole's ingenuity. “Ingenuity, as we have seen, was an important element in the piecing together of Strawberry Hill and The Castle of Otranto; but The Castle of Otranto has passed through fifty editions, four within the last nine years, and Strawberry Hill is concluding its second century. “

Lewis was writing in 1934, when Strawberry Hill had become home to a teachers' training college. It is now owned by a Trust, which has restored the building in accordance with Walpole's plans and which now opens it to the public. Aristocrat though he was to the core, one would imagine that Horace would be pleased for ‘the common people’, as he referred to the rest of us, by such a climactic achievement.

View of Chatsworth
After Edward Dayes, Print by R. Pollard, 1794

CHAPTER EIGHTEEN

1760	Until July: London
	July to October: Cambridge
	October to following June: London
1761	June: Cambridge
	July: Tour in Suffolk
	July to September: Cambridge
	September to November: London.
1762	Until March: Cambridge
	March to May: London
	July to November: York and Old Park
	Early November: Journey to London (Tour including **Chatsworth**)
	November: London
	Late November to following May: Cambridge

There are stretches of Gray's life where it is difficult to find any events to record and one is tempted to say, as Gosse did of this year (1762), 'Nothing could be more humdrum than Gray's existence about this time.' There is no sign of literary life in him and the whole year seems only broken by a journey northwards in the summer. Towards the end of June he went to stay at York for a fortnight with Mason, whose 'insatiable avarice', as Gray calls it in writing to him, had been lulled for a little while by the office of residentiary [canon] of York Cathedral....From York Gray went on to Durham, to stay with Wharton at Old Park, where he was extremely happy; 'we take in no newspaper or magazine, but the cream and butter are beyond compare'. He made a long stay, and rather late in the autumn set out for a tour of Yorkshire by himself.....After passing through Chesterfield and Mansfield, Gray descended the Trent, spent two or three days at Nottingham, and came up to London by the coach. He reported back to Wharton later (in December) in a letter from Cambridge.

> Dear Doctor,
> I feel very ungrateful every day, that I continue silent, & yet I do not write to you: but now the pen is on my hand, and I am in for it. when I left you, in spite of the rain I went out of my way to Richmond, and made a shift to see the Castle, & look down the

valley, through which the Swale winds: that was all the weather would permit. at Rippon I visited the Church, which we had neglected before, with some pleasure, and saw the Ure full to its brink & very inclinable to overflow. some faint gleams of sunshine gave me an opportunity of walking over Studley, and descending into the ruins of Fountain's Abbey, which I examined with attention. I passed over the ugly moor of Harrowgate, made a bow to the Queen's Head, and got late at night to Leeds: here the rain was so perverse I could scarce see the town, much less go to Kirkstall Abbey, wch was my intention; so I proceeded to Wakefield, & Wentworth Castle. here the Sun again indulged me, and open'd a as beautiful a scene of rich & cultivated country, as (I am told) Yorkshire affords. the water is all artificial, but with an air of nature; much wood; a very good house in the Q: Anne style, wch is now new-fronting in a far better taste by the present Earl[55]; many pictures not worth a farthing, & a castle built only for a plaything on the top of the hill as a point of view, & to command a noble prospect. I went on to Sheffield, liked the situation in a valley by a pretty river's side, surrounded with charming hills: saw the handsome parish church with the chapel & monuments of the Talbots. then I entered the Peak, a countrey beyond comparison uglier than any other I have seen in England, black, tedious, barren, & not mountainous enough to please one with its horrors. this is mitigated, since you were there by a road like a bowling-green, which soon brought me to Chatsworth. the house has the air of a palace, the hills rising on three of its sides shut out the view of its dreary neighbourhood, & are covered with wood to their tops: the front opens to the Derwent winding thro' the valley, which, by the art of Mr Brown[56] is now always

---

[55] William Wentworth (1722-91), second Earl of Strafford.

[56] Lancelot Brown (1715-83), commonly known as Capability Brown.

> visible & full to its brim. for heretofore it could not well be seen (but in rainy seasons) from the windows. a handsome bridge is lately thrown over it, & the stables taken away, wch stood full in view between the house & the river. the prospect opens here to a wider tract of country terminated by more distant hills: this scene is yet in its infancy, the objects are thinly scatter'd, & the clumps and plantations lately made, but it promises well in time. within doors the furniture corresponds to the stateliness of the apartments, fine tapestry, marble doorcases with fruit, flowers, and foliage, excellently done by Old Cibber's Father, windows of plate glaſs in gilded frames, & such a profusion of Gibbons' best carving in wood, viz. Dead-Game, fish, shells, flowers, &c. as I never saw anywhere. the cielings and staircases all painted by Verrio or Laguerre, in their usual sprawling way, & no other pictures, but in one room 8 or 10 portraits, some of them very good, of James & Charles the first's time. the gardens are small, & in the French style; with water-works, particularly a grand Cascade of steps, & a *Temple d'eaux* at the head of it. from thence I went to Hardwick. one would think Mary Queen of Scots, was but just walked down into the Park with her guard for half-an-hour. her gallery, her room of audience, her anti-chamber, with the very canopies, just as she left them. a little tatter'd indeed, but the more venerable; & all preserved with religious care, & paper'd up in winter. the park & country are just like Hertfordshire. I went by Chesterfield & Mansfield to revisit my old friend the Trent at Nottingham, where I passed 2 or 3 days, & from thence took stage-coach to London.

Gray's first reaction to Chatsworth was to be stunned. 'The house has the air of a Palace….' The present Duchess of Devonshire disagrees. 'The building….is not a palace, not a castle, not a museum but a house…' She goes on to try to define its spirit. 'Chatsworth is in a valley in the Peak District of Derbyshire, high up and in the middle of England. It is a very big house in a very big valley, with a steep and wooded hill behind, a river in front, encompassed by a large garden and even larger park: the usual receipt for a English country house....But there is a quality about the place which makes it out of the ordinary. Perhaps the giant scale has something to do with it, or perhaps it is the scenery, a classic mixture of wild and domestic: moor, rocks and bracken descending through woods to grazing land and quiet riverside....The house looks permanent - as permanent as if it had been there not for a few hundred years but for ever. It fits the landscape exactly. The river is the right distance away and the right width. The bridge is at a comfortable angle for leaning on and gazing from. The stone from which the house is built comes out of the ground nearby, and so it is the proper colour ....This distant enclosure [within blocks of trees] gives an impression of a secure place beyond which the unknown world may be ugly and badly arranged, but within the magic boundary all is well.'

Gray visited at an important time for the house. Change was under way. As he remarks, 'a handsome bridge is lately thrown over it'[the Derwent]. The present Duchess appears to be particularly proud of this bridge. 'The new bridge of 1762 is entirely satisfying in make and shape, but it is the oblique angle at which it stands that sets it apart...Was it Paine or his patron who decided that it should stand at forty degrees to the West Front? As a result, the bridge is placed at just the correct angle for leaning on and gazing from, and in that decision lies the genius'.

What was also changing was the stables, which Gray notes have been 'taken away'. By 1765 they had been replaced with the magnificent structure that is there now, 'one of the most beautiful ranges of stables in this country', with stalls for eighty horses, now finding room for a restaurant.

Gray's tour 'within doors' fastens on memorable items, such as Cibber's work and that of Grinling Gibbons. To quote the Duchess again, on the Chapel this time, she has guidance for Gray. 'The only painting by Verrio in the chapel is *St Thomas' Incredulity*,1693, over the altar. The walls and the ceiling were the work of Louis Laguerre. A recent discovery is his signature, 'L. Laguer' scratched into the ragged fringe of dark cloth behind the legs of the figures on the west wall; and there is no proof that the carving is by Gibbons'. She goes on with more exact information. 'The incomparable Cibber, the stone carver who worked at Chatsworth from 1688 to 1691, designed the altarpiece and carved the figures of Faith and Justice. The whole is executed in Derbyshire alabaster and flanked by a pair of black Ashford marble pillars. Another pair support the gallery opposite. The draped swags, festoons, urns and cherubs are the work of Derbyshire-born Watson, whose huge output and contribution to Chatsworth are second to none. His carving in stone, marble and wood adorns most of the grand rooms in the house'[57].

Gray was also wrong about Hardwick. Mary Queen of Scots was executed three years before the building of Hardwick Hall was started. She could not have been imprisoned there and Gray's day-dream about walking in the park and feeling her presence in the audience chamber was based on a mistake. It is true that there is a Mary Queen of Scots room at Hardwick but that seems to be a bait for tourists; it suited the family for years to encourage the legend about Mary's stay in the house. But it is not like Gray to make a simple historical mistake.

[57] Duchess of Devonshire, *Chatsworth: The House*, London: Frances Lincoln, 2002, p.106.

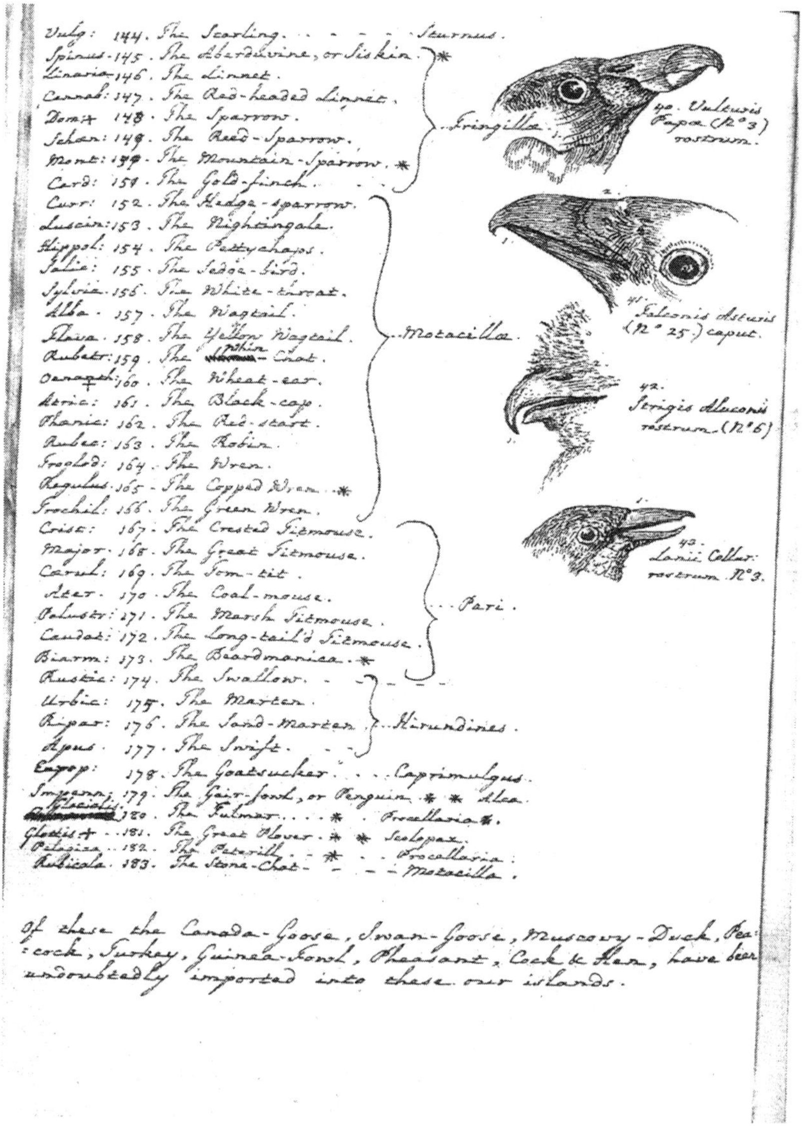

Vulg: 144. The Stearling. . . . . Sturnus.
Spinus. 145. The Aberdavine, or Siskin. *
Linaria. 146. The Linnet.
Cannab: 147. The Red-headed Linnet.
Dom: 148. The Sparrow.
Schoen: 149. The Reed-Sparrow.
Mont: 150. The Mountain-Sparrow. *
Card: 151. The Gold-finch.
. . Fringilla.

Curr: 152. The Hedge-sparrow.
Luscin: 153. The Nightingale.
Hippol: 154. The Pettychaps.
Salic: 155. The Sedge-bird.
Sylvia. 156. The White-throat.
Alba. 157. The Wagtail.
Flava. 158. The Yellow Wagtail.
Rubetr: 159. The ~~[illegible]~~ Whin-Chat.
Oenanth: 160. The Wheat-ear.
Atric: 161. The Black-cap.
Phoenic: 162. The Red-start.
Rubec: 163. The Robin.
Troglod: 164. The Wren.
Regulus. 165. The Copped Wren. *
Trochil: 166. The Green Wren.
. . Motacilla.

Crist: 167. The Crested Titmouse.
Major. 168. The Great Titmouse.
Caerul: 169. The Tom-tit.
Ater. 170. The Coal-mouse.
Palustr: 171. The Marsh Titmouse.
Caudat: 172. The Long-tail'd Titmouse.
Biarm: 173. The Beardmanica. *
. . Pari.

Rustic: 174. The Swallow.
Urbic: 175. The Martin.
Ripar: 176. The Sand-martin.
Apus. 177. The Swift.
. . Hirundines.

Europ: 178. The Goatsucker. . . . Caprimulgus.
Impenn: 179. The Gair-fowl, or Penguin * * Alca.
Glacialis 180. The Fulmar . . . * . Procellaria *.
Gladis . . 181. The Great Plover . * * Scolopax.
Pelagica . . 182. The Peterill . * . . Procellaria.
Rubicola. 183. The Stone-Chat . . . . Motacilla.

Of these the Canada-Goose, Swan-Goose, Muscovy-Duck, Pea:cock, Turkey, Guinea-Fowl, Pheasant, Cock & Hen, have been undoubtedly imported into these our islands.

A Page from one of Gray's Notebooks

CHAPTER NINETEEN

1763 To May: Cambridge.
May to June: London, with 'a little jaunt to Epsom and Boxhill'.
June to September: Cambridge.
Sept to October: 'a little ramble away from Cambridge'.
October to November: Cambridge.
November to December: London.

(A) Algarotti

Gray's circle of acquaintances among other learned men of his age and society was limited. He tended to keep out of the way of meeting people of national or international importance. An exception occurred in the spring of 1763 when he came into contact, albeit at a distance, with the then famous Count Algarotti. Algarotti was a man of many talents. In the words of the Britannica article, 'his urbanity, his brilliant conversation, his good looks, and his versatile intelligence made an impression on intellectuals, such as Voltaire.... and eventually on Frederick the Great'. To be noticed by Algarotti was therefore something of an achievement. Gray owed this notice to an acquaintance from Pembroke, William How. How had first appeared at Pembroke in 1751; after leaving for a legal career in Lincoln's Inn he was re-admitted to Pembroke as a fellow-Commoner in 1758 and Gray must have got to know him then. How travelled in Italy, met Algarotti, and in the course of the meeting presented Algarotti with a volume of Gray's poetry. Algarotti was duly impressed and wrote to Gray in extravagant terms, presenting him with a number of his own works and sending a set of his works to Pembroke College. Gray's reaction is decidedly mixed: undoubtedly pleased, but also a little satirical at the style of 'superlative panegyric' (to quote Mason, who also received Algarotti's commendation). After addressing his letter to 'illustrissimo Signor Signor Padrone Colendissimo '[most revered], Algarotti had gone on to compare Gray to Pindar. After some delay (five months) Gray replied politely and at some length on the subject of the reunification of the arts of music, poetry and dance. He took the occasion to include an anecdote about a performance of a Burletta which he [Gray] had attended, at which a young singer had distinguished herself with ' the utmost justness of ear, the strongest expression of countenance, the most speaking eyes, the greatest vivacity & variety of gesture' (already referred to in Chapter 2, page 22). Undoubtedly Gray was recalling a great moment in his own listening experience; what Algarotti would make of so personal an anecdote we will never know. Algarotti died the next year in Pisa.

Gray wrote to Brown initially, in February, when he first heard from How about the Algarotti meeting, and wrote again in August to Wharton to describe some of his reactions.

> Mason and I have received letters from Count Algarotti, *Chamberlan de sa Majesté le Roi de Pruſse*, with observations (that is, panegyricks) on our Tragedies & our Odes, & a present of certain Italian Diſsertations, wch he has lately publish'd on the state of painting and music. one of them is dedicated to Mr Pitt, whom he styles - *Unno immortale, e Restitutore d'Inghilterra, Amico del gran Federigo.....*

Gray chooses to treat this tribute in a frivolous way but he did quickly acquire an international reputation, of which this is the beginning. The *Elegy* has been translated into a number of different languages [the British Library has versions in Italian, French, German, Greek, Portuguese, and Welsh] and there have been good studies of Gray's achievement by French, German, and Italian critics.

(B) Nature Notes

Gray continued this letter to Wharton with a typical list of nature notes, which are worth the transcribing and examining in some detail.

> I kept an exact account of Heat & Cold in the Spring here: the sum & substance of wch is, that (at 9 in the morning) on the 18th of January, the Therm: was at 31, & the small birds were so tame you might take them up with your hand. this was the greatest cold. on the 15th April it was at 58, & the same afternoon at 65, wch was the greatest heat from Jan: 1 to May 1st.

Feb.	3.	Snowdrops flower'd
...	12	Crocus & Hepatica fl:, the snow then lieing, & Therm: at 45.
...	18	Chaffinch sings. Bees appear.
...	21	White butterfly abroad.
...	25	Gnats flie, & large flies. Mezereon fl:
...	27	Honeysuckle & Gooseberry unfold their leaves.
March	1	Violet flowers (in the garden). Rose opens its leaf..
...	3	Daffodil & single Hyacinth fl: Spider spins.
...	5	Thrush singing.
...	6	Elder in leaf, Currant & Weeping Willow in l:
...	8	Apricot blows. Sky-Lark singing.
...	11	Wind very high at S:E:, wch continued with hard frost.
...	16	Frost gone.
...	18	Abricot in full bloom.
...	19	Almond flowers. Lilac, Barberry, & Gelder-rose in leaf.
April	2	Standard Abricot, & Wall-Pears flower. Quince, Apple,and Sweet-briar in leaf. Currant flowers. Dutch-Elm opens its leaf.
...	4	Plumb in leaf.
...	5	Crown imperial fl:

...	6	Plumb flowers. Hawthorn, Horse-Chestnut, Mountain-Ash, in leaf.
...	9	Lime-tree in leaf. Jonquil & single Anemone flower. Lady-birds seen.
...	11	Cowslip flowers, & Auricula. Swallow appears. young Rooks caw in the nest.
...	14	Red-start appears. Cherries in full bloom.
...	15	Frontignac Vine in leaf. Double Wall-flower blows.
...	16	Nightingale sings. Apple blossoms.
...	19	Chaffinch & Red-Start sit on their eggs.
...	20	Elm, Willow, & Ash in flower (with the Black-thorn). Hawthorn in full leaf.
...	21	Sycomore quite green. Oak puts out.

Pray present my respects to Mrs & Miſs Wharton.
I am ever, Sincerely Yours.

Gray writes, not only with the eye of the poet but also with the knowledge of the naturalist, and the scientifiically-trained naturalist at that. As Alastair Macdonald puts it in his poem on Gray, he is the 'unacknowledged poet of field and wood, temperatures and weathers, whose eye incised appearance and behaviour with ageless, lucid words'. His vocabulary and his reservoir of knowledge are wider in range than ours. 'Mezereon', for instance, is now a national rarity; Gray records its flowering as a matter of course, as Gilbert White did. According to Richard Mabey (*Flora Britannica*, p. 234), it 'was widely planted close to cottage doors' perhaps because of the 'heady fragrance of its February flowers'. Similarly, Gray could spot the frontignac vine, presumably on a college garden hot-wall, before the days of the university botanical garden, and knew that the berberis shrub, that we now plant in gardens (beneath the window) to deter burglars, was worth cultivating for its barberries, no longer eaten in the west. Gray's dates and timings are interesting too, in view of global warming and its disturbance of the times of arrival of the swallow - now rather earlier than Gray's April 11 date (24 March recorded in 2010) - and the appearance of the first butterflies and bees. Gray must also have had some elementary recording instruments for his temperatures and wind directions. He is interested in the gnat, the spider, and the ladybird, as well as the nightingale and the sky-lark, and a wide range of trees (elm, willow, ash, horse-chestnut, hawthorn, elder and almond). And there are, interestingly, a few odd word-usages not known to the *Oxford English Dictionary*: the oak 'puts out' (goes into leaf?) and the double wall-flower 'blows' (blossoms?). One wonders how many of today's literary critics, who dissect his poetry, also have Gray's background of botanical knowledge. This is not an academic point: what is at issue is Gray's status as a polymath - a person whose expertise spans a significant number of different subject areas - and that affects one's attitude to his poetic and literary achievement.

These nature notes occur at frequent intervals in his letters and are always interesting, sometimes for their contrast with twenty-first century data for similar periods of time, sometimes for the terms which Gray uses, sometimes for the minutiae of his observations. Gray was taking thermometer readings every day and had some sort of anemometer to give him wind directions. He was exchanging these observations with Wharton, who (he implies) was keeping notes according to a similar system for comparison purposes. In his library he could refer to Thomas Pennant, John Ray, Gilbert White, and, of course, Linnaeus, whose *Systema Naturae* he heavily annotated. C.E. Norton summed up his conclusions from studying these annotations (repeated from p.114): 'The work which these volumes exhibit is so remarkable a monument to Gray's learning and industry, and throws so much light on his occupations and interests, especially during the last ten years of his life, that some knowledge of it seems essential, not only to the understanding of the course of his days, but even more to a just appreciation of his character and his acquisitions'[58].

The following is a similar extract from an earlier letter, written to Wharton in September, 1759.

> I do not see much myself of the face of nature here, but I enquire. Wheat was cutting in Kent the 23[d] of July, the 25th at Enfield. the 27th Wheat, Barley, & Oats cutting all at once about Windsor: the forward Pease all got in, ground plough'd and turneps sow'd. 9th of August Harvest still continued in Buck:[re]. the 27th about Kennington it was

[58] C.E. Norton, *The Poet Gray as a Naturalist*, Boston, 1903.

> just over, being delay'd for want of hands. In some places 50 mile from London it is but just over now for the same reason. the 3[d] of Aug: Catherine-pears, Muscle-plums[59], & small black Cherries were sold in wheelbarrows. Filberds[60] in plenty the 8th. Mulberries, & fine green-gage plums, the 19th. Fine Nectarines & Peaches, the 27th. the 4th of Sept:[r] Melons & Perdrigon-plums[61]. the 8th, Walnuts 20 a penny. this is all I know about fruit. my weather is not very compleat.
>
> ....
>
> I go no further than you do: but it is down in my book....
> Yours, T.G. Southampton-Row, Sept. 18. 1759

In fact, Gray continued his data, not the most riveting reading, perhaps, to the end of August. He seems to have enjoyed a good warm dry spell, at least till the end of the month. He ends this page of notes with a record of a 'moonshiny night', which sounds like a harvest moon. The earlier data about harvesting gives a lovely picture of rural London, harvesting in Enfield and Kennington, if you please, and of cherries by the wheel-barrow load and of walnuts at 20 a penny. These passages - and they can be found all over the place in notebooks and in marginalia - make enchanting reading.

---

[59] An old variety of plum, used for baking and preserving.
[60] A type of edible hazel-nut.
[61] An old variety of culinary plum from the south of France.

Schiehallion from Wade's Road above Calvine
[Photograph by the author]

CHAPTER TWENTY

1764	Till May: Cambridge
	May to June: London
	June to September: Cambridge.
	September to October: Winchester, Stonehenge, etc.
	October to November: London
	November to following April Cambridge.
1765	Previous November to April: Cambridge.
	April to May: London, with visit to Windsor.
	May to August: York, Old Park, Hartlepool.
	18 Aug. to 7 Oct: journey to Glamis, with **Excursion to Highlands.**
	7 October to 14 October: return Journey by Perth and Stirling to Old Park
	14 to 28 October: Old Park.
	October to December: London.

This is the year of Gray's epic journey to Scotland, a journey later eclipsed by the Lake quest for the sublime, the raising of the mental threshold whereby frighten District tour but almost as important in its exploration of wild country and the ing experiences became inspiring.

Gray certainly started with all the English prejudices about Scottish primitiveness. He expected and, of course, found poor standards of housing, unhealthy inns with unappetising food, dangerous and poorly kept roads. In a note to his friend Brown he included the following advice: 'See your sheets air'd yourself. Eat mutton or hard eggs. Touch no fried things'. It took him three days from Old Park to reach Edinburgh, where he was entertained by a group of *literati.* He was apparently so shy and reserved that he gained for himself an undeserved and mistaken reputation for pride. Eventually, after an exciting crossing of the Forth in a four-oared yawl and a night at Perth, he reached Glamis and from the tower of that spectacular castle gained his first view of the magnetic mountain, Schiehallion. He was then taken on a five-day Highland tour by his host, Major Strathmore, and when they reached Kenmore, beyond Dunkeld, they came within view of Schiehallion again. His description of that part of his journey is described in part of a long letter to Dr Wharton, written from Glamis Castle.

....down by the side of the river under the thickest shades is seated the Town of Dunkeld: in the midst of it stands a ruin'd Cathedral, the towers & shell of the building still entire. a little beyond it a large house of the Duke of Athol with its offices & gardens extends a mile beyond the town, & as his grounds were interrupted by the streets & roads he has flung arches of communication acrofs them, that add to the scenery of the place, w[ch] of itself is built of good white stone, & handsomely slated, so that no one would take it for a Scotch Town till they come into it. here we pafs'd the night: if I told you how, you would blefs yourself. next day we set forward to Taymouth 27 miles farther West, the road winding thro' beautiful woods with the Tay almost always in full view to the right, being here from 3 to 400 feet over. The Strath-Tay from a mile to 3 miles or more wide, cover'd with corn & spotted with groups of people then in the midst of their harvest, on either hand a vast chain of rocky mountains, that changed their face & open'd something new every hundred yards, as the way turn'd, or the clouds pafs'd: in short altogether it was one of the most pleasing days I have pafs'd these many years, & at every step I wish'd for you. at the close of day we came to *Balloch.* so the place was call'd: but now for decency *Taymouth,* improperly enough, for here it is, that the river ifsues out of Loch-Tay (a glorious lake 15 miles long & 1½ broad) surrounded with prodigious mountains. there on its N: Eastern brink impending o'er it is the vast hill of Lawers: to the East is that monstrous creature of God, *Shekhallian* (i:e: the Maiden's Pap) spiring above the clouds. directly West (beyond the end of the Lake) *Beni-More* (the Great Mountain) rises to a most aweful height, & looks down on the tomb of Fingal.

The reference to Fingal is prompted by Gray's interest in the Ossianic poems of James Macpherson. These had first come to his attention in April 1760, when half of him worried about their authenticity while the other half enthused about their originality. The following extract from a letter to Wharton written in June 1760 makes clear that enthusiasm tended to take preference over doubt:

> If you have seen Stonehewer, he has probably told you of my old Scotch (or rather Irish) poetry. I am gone mad about them. they are said to be translations (literal and in prose) from the Erse tongue, done by one Macpherson, a young Clergyman in the High-lands. he means to publish a Collection he has of these specimens of antiquity, if it be antiquity: but what plagues me is, I cannot come at any certainty on that head. I was so struck, so *extasié*, with their infinite beauty, that I writ into Scotland to make a thousand enquiries....

Gray was prone to superlatives and *extasié* is one of his most extravagant. He was deeply affected by the tone and nature of the Ossianic poems: this led to a study of Celtic literature with his usual thoroughness and eventually to the composition of *The Bard*, and to this visit to Scotland. It was the Romantic streak in Gray that came to this judgement and this change of area of interest. As Fiona Stafford says, "In Britain, all the great Romantic poets came under Macpherson's spell to a greater or lesser degree.... Ossian was a herald of the Romantic Movement.".

At the end of day one, they stayed the night at what is now called Kenmore but was then called, to Gray's confusion, Balloch, crossed the Tummel, and set out for a walk along General Wade's Military road. Gray found the experience frightening, horribly beautiful, mixing fear with excitement.

> we ferried over the Tummel in order to get into Marshal Wade's road (wch leads from Dunkeld to Invernefs) & continued our way along it toward the North. the road is excellent, but dangerous enough in conscience. the river often running directly under us at the bottom of a precipice 200 feet deep, sometimes masqued indeed by wood, that finds means to grow where I could not stand: but very often quite naked & without any defence. in such

places we walked for miles together partly for fear, & partly to admire the beauty of the country, wch the beauty of the weather set off to the greatest advantage. as evening came on, we approach'd the Pafs of Gillikrankie, where in the year 45 the Hefsians with their Prince at their head stop'd short, & refused to march a foot farther. *Vestibulum ante ipsum, primisq infaucibus Orci*[77] stands the solitary mansion of Mr Robinson of Fascley. close by it rises a hill cover'd with oak, with grotesque mafses of rock staring from among their trunks, like the sullen countenances of Fingal & all his family frowning on the little mortals of modem days. from between this hill and the adjacent mountains pent in a narrow channel comes roaring out the river Tummel, & falls headlong down involved in white foam wch rises into a mist all round it - but my paper is deficient, & I must say nothing of the Pafs itself, the black river Garry, the Blair of Athol, Mount Beni-Gloe, my return (by another road) to Dunkeld, the Hermitage, the *Stra-Brann* & the Rumbling-Brigg. in short since I saw the Alps, I have seen nothing sublime till now....

The name of the village at which Gray stayed, with which he had so much difficulty, was originally Balloch. Gray was so squeamish about it, because the name means, testicle (as in the modern slang, 'bollocks'). Not surprisingly, that name was superseded by the more polite Taymouth, and more recently by Kenmore. Inhabitants of the Balloch on Loch Lomond can relax, as that derivation is different: from 'bealach', meaning pass.

This mountain, 'She-khallian' as Gray spelt it, clearly fascinated Gray. He could see it from Glamis; he saw it again from Taymouth. Somebody had told him that the Gaelic name meant 'The Maiden's Pap', a name he clearly felt a little coy about, but the meaning preferred by the SMC Guide to Hill Names is the 'fairy hill of the Caledonians', Perthshire being the heartland of the Caledonian tribes. As for its spelling, it has, not surprisingly, varied

[77] *Aeneid* VI. 273. "Right before the entrance, in the very jaws of Orcus"

considerably over the years: in 1642 it appears as 'Schahalzean'. It is, of course, an iconic mountain, in the sense of being famous from its shape and its visibility from so many places right round the compass. It is a hill that you can see from 50 miles away, from the other side of Rannoch Moor, for instance, way to the west, and from Ben Vrackie above Pitlochry over to the east. It also has a history. The regularity of its cone-like shape (which permitted a reasonably accurate determination of its volume) attracted the 18th century Astronomer Royal, Neil Maskelyne, who conducted experiments in 1774 on its flanks to derive the earth's mass. The apparent difference of latitude between two stations on opposite sides of the mountain was compared with the real difference of latitude obtained by triangulation. From Maskelyne's observations Charles Hutton deduced a density for the earth 4.5 times that of water; the modern value is 5.515.

The real point of interest about Schiehallion, however, is Gray's description of it as 'that monstrous creature of God'. Much can be read into this remarkable phrase. There are mountains which have a dark and brooding presence, which might account for a feeling of fear. It is a common reaction to the Eiger, for instance, and one might feel daunted by the massiveness of the north face of Ben Nevis. I remember well the feeling that overwhelmed me one night in the Himalayas when a huge stone-fall crashed and thundered across the glacier on which my tent was placed, generating a vision of evil, blind, destructive force. It is something of this kind that Gray is trying to suggest with the oxymoron, the apparent contradiction in the two parts of the phrase, "monstrous" and God-created. One would not now have expected it of Schiehallion. Most people now react to Schiehallion's perfect conical/triangular shape as making a perfect picture. Gray, however, clearly felt a combination of awe and fear: he sensed that it could be dangerous at the same time as feeling God's presence as its creator. It is something akin to Blake's sense of the tiger's 'fearful symmetry'. It is a feeling that prefigures Romantic animism, Wordsworth's God in Nature, but it is clearly not a comfortable feeling.

I tried to imagine Gray's feeling when standing on the military road, as I stood on it above Calvine looking across to Schiehallion - but I got the width of the road wrong.

The waters roared below: his nerves to calm,
Gray pleaded with the major: 'Take my arm!'
'Stop thinking of those Hessians!' came the reply.
The road curved upwards under a fatal sky:
No parapet to bridges and barely five foot wide,
Thumped flat by soldiers' sledges - no place to bide.
A kaleidoscope of hill-shapes 'gainst the sky appeared,
Among them a peak, black, huge, triangular, up-reared.
'My God!' he cried. 'What monstrous symmetry!'
Transported out of diffidence by sharp sublimity.

Gray's summarizing sentence - 'in short since I saw the Alps, I have seen nothing sublime till now' - is a particularly important one, since the search for the sublime was to become so intrinsic to the Romantic experience. Crossing the Alps by the Mont Cenis pass and visiting the Grand Chartreuse had been life-changing experiences for the young Gray and they were to animate his explorations not only of Scotland but later also of the Lake District. They condition what he is looking for in wild scenery and explain the therapeutic and spiritual benefit of this kind of travel. A pity that it all had to end with the 'itch' of bed bugs in Edinburgh!

Portrait of William Mason,
Etching, after Lewis Vaslet, c. 1771

CHAPTER TWENTY-ONE

1766	Until April: Cambridge.
	April to May: London
	May to July: Canterbury, Marsgate, Dover.
	July: London.
	July to September: Cambridge.
	September: Suffolk and Norfolk.
	September to October Cambridge.
	October to December: London.
1767.	December to April: Cambridge
	April to June: London with trip to Strawberry Hill
	May: **Death of Mary, the wife of Gray's friend, William Mason**
	June: Cambridge
	June to July: Aston, with trip to Dovedale and Peak
	July to October: Old Park, with visits to Rokeby, Keswick, etc.
	October: York
	November and December: London.

At some stage, probably earlier than this, most biographers have to come to terms with the way their subject relates to other people, forms personal relationships. We have already seen, in the example of the visit to Edinburgh, how Gray could give offence by seeming stand-offish-ness, how his shyness could be interpreted as conceit or hauteur. Gray's circle of friends and acquaintances was limited, partly by shyness and partly by his choice of a restricted life-style. William Mason was a major figure in the later events of Gray's life but Gray's treatment of him presents problems. Mason was born in Hull in 1725 and went up to Cambridge as a pensioner at St Johns in 1742. He first became acquainted with Gray in 1747 and possibly by Gray's influence was elected a fellow of Pembroke in that year. He made various attempts to establish himself as a writer, publishing an Anglo-Saxon story called *Elfrida* in 1752. When his father died in 1753, he needed to find a replacement source of income and managed to get himself ordained as a priest and then initiated as rector of Aston near York in 1754. Gray helped Mason with careful and meaningful suggestions in the composition of *Caractacus* (published 1755), even though he must have been painfully aware of the dullness and mediocrity of the material he was reading. Mason married a Mary Sherman in 1765 but she died two years later to Mason's considerable grief. When Gray died in 1771 Mason and James Brown acted as Gray's executors and so he was responsible for the preservation and publication of Gray's complete works and of his letters, though he did resort to some censorship in the case of the letters. The rest of his life was filled with various further attempts at authorship, notably including the long poem *The English Garden* and he continued to seek preferment. He led a busy social life and helped to raise funds for the impecunious and improvident Christopher Smart. With Stonehewer and Brown, he was responsible for the monument to Gray in Westminster Abbey in 1778. Mason died at Aston in April 1797.

When Mason's wife, Mary, died in May of 1767, Gray wrote to Mason immediately he heard of the news, in the following words.

> I break in upon you at a moment, when we least of all are permitted to disturb our friends, only to say, that you are daily & hourly present to my thoughts. if the worst be not yet past: you will neglect & pardon me. but if the last struggle be over: if the poor object of our long anxieties be no longer sensible to your kindneſs, or to her own sufferings: allow me (at least in idea, for what could I do, were I present, more than this?) to sit by you in silence, & pity from my heart not her, who is at rest; but you, who lose her. may he, who made us, the master of our pleasures, & of our pains, preserve & support you! Adieu.[55]

There is no doubting the sincerity of Gray's sympathy or the tactfulness and sense of what he says by way of consolation, or sharing of sorrow. In this crisis Gray reveals the true nature of his relationship with William Mason, a sharing of emotion at a personal level. There were, however, times when Gray treated Mason with far less respect and it is instructive to place this letter of real emotion alongside the words which Gray wrote when Mason announced his intention to marry a few years earlier in [October] 1763.

---

[55] *(Note from Correspondence)* In the blank space at the end of the letter... Mason has appended the following note: 'the voice of Friendship in its tenderest & most pathetic note...'

> I rejoice but has she common sense, is she a gentlewoman? has she money? has she a nose? I know she sings a little, & twiddles on the harpsichord, hammers at sentiment, & puts herself in an attitude, admires a cast in the eye, & can say Elfrida by heart: but these are only the virtues of a Maid. do let her have some wife-like qualities, & a double portion of prudence, as she will have not only herself to govern, but you also, & that with an absolute sway. your Friends, I doubt not, will suffer for it: however we are very happy, & have no other wish than to see you settled in the world. we beg you would not stand fiddleing about it, but be married forthwith, & then take chaise, and come consummating all the way to Cambridge to be touch'd by Mr Brown, & so to London, where to be sure she must paſs the first winter. if good reasons (& not your own, not her coquetry) forbid this: yet come hither yourself, for our Copuses [beer-cups, tankards] and Welch Rabbits are impatient for you.

It was not a very tactful letter, certainly, nor even a kind one, but written from a certain kind of bachelor sense of humour which one may not like much but has to allow in some situations. Not, however, so bad as to justify the criticism bestowed up on it by Lytton Sells, one of Gray's biographers, who labels it 'perhaps the unkindest letter he ever wrote'. What really upset Lytton Sells was the coarse remark – often omitted from printed versions of the letter – which he describes as 'a grossly indecent suggestion as to how the couple should proceed on their honeymoon journey'. Even in 1980, when Lytton Sells was writing, this was surely a very harsh judgement. Robert Mack, in his recent biography of Gray, is surely right to see this letter in a different light. 'Gray's playfulness may sound a bit too misogynistic in our ears today but his fooling at least highlights the slightly more caustic side of his character and of his peculiar brand of wit'. Nobody now is surely going to be outraged by the word 'consummating' , though it is interesting that this letter is omitted from the Worlds Classics edition of Gray's letters in 1925. What may be complained of is Gray's rough condescension towards Mason, which is evident in other letters.

Gray apparently nicknamed Mason Scroddles: 'affectionately dubbed' is how Mack sees it. The name is certainly an advance in familiarity from the Latinisms of the Quadruple Alliance, but it is hardly a term of respect. Gray seems always to have looked down on Mason and taken his useful friendship on trust. But the first letter shows Gray's real underlying feeling and tenderness and kindness, in its tactful and sensitive reaction to the young Mrs Mason's sad and untimely death.

We owe a lot to William Mason but he has not been well repaid by posterity. George Saintsbury's verdict on Mason was that he was 'one of the paltriest and most pretentious poet-tasters who ever trespassed on the English Parnassus'. The DNB [author: Jules Smith], however, makes the point that 'Mason did not have a unified identity'. He did make a considerable contribution to gardening history, planning the restoration of the gardens at Nuneham Courtenay for Lord Harcourt - "one of the most beautiful in Britain"i - and he was also he was also an accomplished musician, playing several keyboard instruments and collaborating with Giardini, Boyce and Avison. It is too easy to under-estimate Mason; and " as a poet of at least historical importance, he still awaits resurrection."

Playing a similar role as stalwart friend, but different in almost all other respects, is the character of Dr Thomas Wharton. We know almost nothing about Wharton and he remains a shadowy figure. This does not lessen his importance as the one person to whom Gray appears to have felt he could express himself freely. Wharton was the acquaintance of choice when Gray decided to make a journey to the Lakes and it is Wharton to whom he writes his most unguarded letters and it is at Old Park, Wharton's home, in its relaxed domesticity, that Gray seems to have felt most at ease. Small touches, little asides, reveal this comfortable relationship. 'My best compliments to Mrs Wharton & the young ladies (including herself).....''My best compliments to Mrs Wharton; I hear her butter is the best in the Bishoprick'.... or this confession: 'Whatever my pen may do, I am sure my thoughts expatiate nowhere oftener or with more pleasure than to Old-Park'. Gray may not have been much of a seeker after married bliss for himself but he appears to have enjoyed the domestic pleasures of the Wharton family and have come back to them repeatedly.

What is also at issue here is Gray's toughness and realism and it is useful to compare his attitudes to Mason and Wharton with his judgements on people in the public eye. It comes as a shock to read the bluntness and acerbity of the criticisms he is capable of making, the sharply satirical streak which is suddenly revealed in poems like *The Candidate*. This poem was circulated slightly surreptitiously in 1764 and was a forthright attack on Lord Sandwich, candidate for the post of High Steward of the university. Sandwich evidently deserved every insult that he got but the main issue with the poem is its attack on the Divinity school in the university, supposedly in favour of Sandwich's election.

> What a pother is here about wenching and roaring!
> Why David loved catches and Solomon whoring.
> Did not Israel filch from the Egyptians of old
> Their jewels of silver and jewels of gold?
> The prophet of Bethel, we read, told a lie;
> He drinks: so did Noah; he swears; so do I.
> To refuse him for such peccadiloes were odd;
> Besides he repents, and he talks about God.
> 'Never hang down your head, you poor penitent elf!
> Come, buss me, I'll be Mrs Twitcher myself.
> Damn ye both for a couple of Puritan bitches!
> He's Christian enough that repents and that stitches[56].

This is surely another case where modern sensibilities are less prone to shock or moral-adjustment-failure. The last line, with its strong slang meaning of 'lying with a woman', shows Gray fully aware of the sexual impulse in all its bawdy interference with legal marital relationships. By the strength of his vocabulary Gray succeeds in vilifying Sandwich in a way that apparently rocked Cambridge at the time. Gray is revealed as considerably more forthright than the quiet image created, say, by David Cecil, but none the worse for that, indeed, better, and far more interesting.

To understand the poem, and Gray's position and attitude, we need to know that in May 1762 Newcastle fell from power and the following year, as

[56] 'Stitch': 'a nickname for a taylor ; also a term for lying with a woman'; Francis Grose, *A Classical Dictionary of the Vulgar Tongue*, London: S.Hooper, 1785

a consequence of Lord Hardwicke's falling ill, the post of High Steward in the university of Cambridge had to be filled by re-election. John Montague, Earl of Sandwich, proposed himself for the vacancy and secured the support of the government of Lord Greville. Sandwich was a notorious profligate, totally unsuitable for such a post, and Gray, who had known Sandwich at Eton, was outraged. Norton Nicholls, in his later reminiscences, declares that 'In the contest for the High Stewardship at Cambridge between Lord Hardwicke and Lord Sandwich Mr Gray took a warm and eager part'. It is Roger Lonsdale's estimate that these lines on The Candidate were written between January and March of 1764. As Lonsdale goes on to say, the lines were not published; 'it is more likely that Gray merely passed the poem round in MS to a few friends and that the fly-sheet was printed much later'. The personification of Sandwich as Jeremy Twitcher is a reference to the cunning and treacherous highwayman in *The Beggar's Opera*, whose 'enduring notoriety' made the nickname appropriate.

A view of Derwentwater towards Borrodale
William Bellers

CHAPTER TWENTY -TWO

1768	To April: Cambridge.
	April to July: Ramsgate and other places in Kent.
	July to August: London
	September: Cambridge.
	September to October: Lovingland, Norwich, Newmarket.
	October to November: Cambridge
1769	Previous December to April: Cambridge
	April to May: London.
	May to July: Cambridge.
	Early July: London.
	Late July: York.
	Late July to Late September: Old Park
	29 September to 13 October**: Tour of the Lake District**
	15-22 October: return journey to Cambridge
	October to December: Cambridge

Gray made two attempts to visit the Lake District (as we now know it), the first in 1767, when his friend Dr Wharton developed asthma and had to return, and the second and more successful, though again without Dr Wharton, in 1769. Gray's record of this tour became a classic account of early tourism and must be the most widely known of Gray's prose writings, largely as a result of its being incorporated in the 1770 edition of West's *Guide to the Lakes*.

Gray was writing simply to inform his friend about what he had missed. He was not writing in a tradition of descriptive travel writing and so the passage lacks the shape and detail which we now expect of this kind of writing: there is none of the logistical detail which weighs down modern guide-book writing: information about mileage, condition of the footpath, distances, transport, availability of refreshment, direction-finding. What we have is a simple narrative enlivened by anecdote and image or pictograph.

Gray's original script went into a notebook, which is now part of the Murray archive; Gray then copied the text into three letters to Wharton, when he was faced with the problem of going on his own and letting Wharton know what he had missed. The letters need, of course, to be read in their entirety. Something of Gray's achievement, however, can be gathered from three or four extracts. The crucial day, with the finest and the most controversial of the descriptions, was day four. Gray, with a local guide, un-named, walked from Keswick to Grange in Borrowdale. The account of the first part of this day is as follows.

> **Oct: 3.** W^{d} at S:E:, a heavenly day. rose at seven, & walk'd out under the conduct of my Landlord to *Borrodale*. the graſs was cover'd with a hoar-frost, wch soon melted, & exhaled in a thin blewish smoke. croſsed the meadows obliquely, catching a diversity of views among the hills over the lake & islands, & changing prospect at every ten paces, left *Cockshut*, & Castle-hill (wch we formerly mounted) behind me, & drew near the foot of *Walla-crag*, whose bare & rocky brow, cut perpendicularly down above 400 feet, as I gueſs, awefully overlooks the way: our path here tends to the left, & the ground gently rising, & cover'd with a glade of scattering trees & bushes on the very margin of the water, opens both ways the most delicious view, that my eyes ever beheld. behind you are the magnificent heights of *Walla*-crag; opposite lie the thick hanging woods of Ld Egremont, & *Newland*-valley with green & smiling fields embosom'd in the dark cliffs; to the left the jaws of *Borodale*, with that turbulent Chaos of mountain behind mountain roll'd in confusion; beneath you, & stretching far away to the right, the shining purity of the *Lake*, just ruffled by the breeze enough to shew it is alive, reflecting rocks, woods, fields, & inverted tops of mountains, with the white buildings of *Keswick*, *Crosthwait*-church, & *Skiddaw* for a back-ground at distance. oh Doctor! I never wish'd more for you; & pray think, how the glaſs played its part in such a spot, wch is called *Carf-close-reeds*: I chuse to set down these barbarous names, that any body may enquire on the place, & easily find the particular station, that I mean.

Gray had the good sense to get up early, essential now if one is to have the countryside to oneself, when Nature is fresh and active. Better still if one goes out at night or very early morning or late in the evening, when the sun is rising or setting or the moon is out and the landscape is dramatically different from sunlit normality. So Gray was there to see the frost 'exhaled in a thin blewish smoke' and the lake still enough to reflect 'rocks, woods, fields, & inverted tops of mountains', and for Gray to sense in his most memorable phrase, 'the shining purity of the lake'. No exaggeration here, as Walla Crag certainly does have a cliff-face of 400 feet of verticality, and the word 'awefully' is used in its full sense of inspiring awe and wonder. That word, 'Awefully', may have dated in its usual usage but the phrase 'Jaws of Borrowdale' has found a secure place for itself in modern tourist literature, which should thank Gray for it. Not everyone feels that Gray's influence has been for the good, however. Norman Nicholson criticized Gray for his use of a Claude glass, mentioned here, because it involves turning your back on nature and looking at its reflection. But it is not so different from framing a view in the screen of a digital camera and very similar to a photo taken with one's self on a mobile phone. Gray continues with his description, going further down the valley.

> this scene continues to *Barrow-gate*, & a little farther, paſsing a brook called *Barrow-beck*, we enter'd *Borodale*. the crags named *Lodoor-banks* now begin to impend terribly over your way; & more terribly, when you hear, that three years since an immense maſs of rock tumbled at once from the brow, & and bar'd all acceſs to the dale (for this is the only road) till they could work their way thro' it. luckily no one was paſsing at the time of this fall; but down the side of the mountain & far into the lake lie dispersed the huge fragments of this ruin in all shapes & in all directions. something farther we turn'd aside into a coppice, ascending a little in front of *Lodoor* water-fall. the height appears to be about 200 feet, the quantity of water not great, tho' (these three days excepted) it had rain'd daily in the hills for near two months before: but then the stream was nobly broken, leaping from rock to rock, & foaming with fury. on one side a towering crag, that spired up to equal, if not overtop, the neighbouring cliffs (this lay all in shade & darkneſs) on the other hand a rounder broader

projecting hill shag'd with wood & illumined by the sun, w[ch] glanced sideways on the upper part of the cataract. the force of the water wearing a deep channel in the ground hurries away to join the lake. we descended again, & pasʃ'd the stream over a rude bridge. soon after we came under *Gowder-crag*, a hill more formidable to the eye & to the apprehension than that of *Lodoor*; the rocks atop, deep-cloven perpendicularly by the rains, hanging loose & nodding forwards, seem just starting from their base in shivers: the whole way down & the road on both sides is strew'd with piles of the fragments strangely thrown acroʃs each other & of a dreadful bulk. the place reminds one of those paʃses in the Alps, where the Guides tell you to move on with speed, & say nothing, lest the agitation of the air should loosen the snows above, & bring down a maʃs, that would overwhelm a caravan. I took their counsel here and hasten'd on in silence.

Non ragioniam di lor; ma guarda, e paʃsa! [57]

[Oct:3] The hills here are cloth'd all up their steep sides with oak, ash, birch, holly, &c: some of it has been cut 40 years ago, some within these 8 years, yet all is sprung again green, flourishing, & tall for its age, in a place where no soil appears but the staring rock, & where a man could scarce stand upright.

One needs to realize, when reading this section of Gray's description that at this time the road was not good enough or wide enough to take vehicles and to emphasize what Gray says about the recent rock avalanches. The crag, now a popular climbing crag, does overhang at this point and come close to the road; in other words it would 'impend terribly', if you have reason to be scared that there are still some rocks waiting to come down. Southey might well be scathing about the timidity of some travellers forty years later but by then things had dramatically changed.[58] Lodore Falls, which Gray stopped to explore, later

[57] Let us not speak of them but look and pass on.

[58] Robert Southey, *Letters from England*, London: The Cresset Press, 1951, p. 242: 'the fear of some travellers who had shrunk back from this dreadful entrance into Borrowdale'.

became a pilgrimage objective, partly as a result of John Dalton's early poem, quoted in full in West's Guide.

> Horrors like these at first alarm
> But soon with savage grandeur charm…

They are indeed hidden from view in the woods and are best seen from the top, rather than from below, as Gray approached them. Gray may well seem to have been exaggerating when he recalled the Alpine guides' warning against making a sound that would trigger an avalanche but he was in that frame of mind that reminded him of the experience of grandeur laced with fear that he had experienced years before in the Grande Chartreuse. This problem of caution or timidity or irrational fear becomes more acute as Gray eventually reached Grange – and stopped.

> Met a civil young farmer overseeing his reapers (for it is oat-harvest here) who conducted us to a neat white house in the village of Grange, wch is built on a rising ground in the midst of a valley. round it the mountains form an aweful amphitheatre, & thro' it obliquely runs the Darwent clear as glaʃs, & shewing under it's bridge every trout, that paʃses. beside the village rises a round eminence of rock cover'd entirely with old trees, & over that more proudly towers *Castle-crag*, invested also with wood on its sides, & bearing on its naked top some traces of a fort said to be Roman. by the side of this hill, wch almost blocks up the way, the valley turns to the left & contracts its dimensions, till there is hardly any road but the rocky bed of the river. the wood of the mountains increases & their summits grow loftier to the eye, & of more fantastic forms: among them appear *Eagle's-Cliff, Dove's-nest, Whitedale-pike*, &c: celebrated names in the annals of Keswick. the dale opens out about four miles higher till you come to *Sea-Whaite* (where lies the way mounting the hills to the right, that leads to the *Wadd-mines*) all farther acceʃs is here barr'd to prying Mortals, only there is a little path winding over the Fells,

& for some weeks in the year pasſable to the Dale's-men; but the Mountains know well, that these innocent people will not reveal the mysteries of their ancient kingdom, the reign of Chaos & old Night. only I learn'd, that this dreadful road dividing again leads one branch to *Ravenglas*, & the other to *Hawkshead*.

For me I went no farther than the Farmer's (better than 4 m: from Keswick) at *Grange*: his Mother & he brought us butter, that Siserah would have jump'd at, tho' not in a lordly dish, bowls of milk, thin oaten-cakes, & ale; & we had carried a cold tongue thither with us. our Farmer was himself the Man, that last year plunder'd the Eagle's eirie: all the dale are up in arms on such an occasion, for they lose abundance of lambs yearly, not to mention hares, partridge, grous, &c: he was let down from the cliff in ropes to the shelf of rock, on wch the nest was built, the people above shouting & hollowing to fright the old birds, wch flew screaming round, but did not dare to attack him. he brought off the eaglet (for there is rarely more than one) & an addle egg. the nest was roundish & more than a yard over, made of twigs twisted together. seldom a year paſses but they take the brood or eggs, & sometimes they shoot one, sometimes the other Parent, but the surviver has always found a mate (probably in Ireland) & they breed near the old place. by his description I learn, that this species is the *Erne* (the Vultur *Albicilla* of Linnaeus in his last edition, but in yours *Falco Albicilla*) so consult him & Pennant about it.

Most current opinion is that Gray exaggerates in his description of the valley 'barr'd to prying mortals'. To Norman Nicholson it was 'obviously preposterous' (*The Lakers*, Cicerone, 1995); to Ian Thompson Gray was 'a wally' (*The English Lakes*, Bloomsbuiry, 2010). Of course, Gray could have got further down the valley but he would have been discouraged from getting too near the Wad mines. They were a strategically important source of lead, which had been attacked and would have been guarded. And he is not so far out in saying that there is 'a little path over the fells' that leads over to Wasdale and eventually to Ravenglass and that that path would be closed by snow for more weeks than it is now. He wanted to be impressed, to be scared, if you like, but he certainly was not a 'wally'. As for Gray's other comments, it is good to find him being welcomed by the locals and enjoying butter 'that Siserah would have jumped at' and oat cakes and ale. The eagles, alas, have gone but they will have been there, with their reputation for attacking lambs and hares, not to mention babies in their cots. Gray was well read in Pennant and Linnaeus on the different kinds of eagle. The *vulture allbicella* may well have been a sea eagle or an osprey, ancestors of which still nest not so far away above Bassenthwaite.

> Walk'd leisurely home the way we came, but saw a new landscape: the features were the same in part, but many new ones were disclosed by the mid-day Sun, & the tints were entirely changed. take notice this was the best or perhaps the only day for going up Skiddaw, but I thought it better employ'd: it was perfectly serene, & hot as midsummer.
>
> In the evening walk'd alone down to the Lake by the side of *Crow-Park* after sunset & saw the solemn colouring of night draw on, the last gleam of sunshine fading away on the hill-tops, the deep serene of the waters, & the long shadows of the mountains thrown acroſs them, till they nearly touch'd the hithermost shore. at distance heard the murmur of many waterfalls not audible in the day-time. wish'd for the Moon, but she was *dark to me & silent, hid in her vacant interlunar cave.*

The final part of this day's description, fittingly 'after sunset', suggests that Gray had read the description of Keswick by Dr John Brown, which was arguably the first description of anywhere in the Lake District in Romantic terms and which finished with a poem written on the top of Walla Crag, describing the moon rising and the silence, which was almost audible. Gray was looking for the same experience of the uncanny: he heard the waterfalls 'not audible in the day time' but was disappointed in the non-appearance of the moon.

There were other days in the tour, which were also revelatory: the evening when he walked up to Crosthwaite Vicarage and saw 'the sweetest scene I can yet discover in point of pastoral beauty'; and the day on which he passed by Grasmere and observed it from the road above, 'this little unsuspected paradise' where 'all is peace, rusticity & happy poverty' . That has left a target phrase for any tourist objective to try to live up to, even if Grasmere now fails so miserably. And the tour ends with a noteworthy visit to Gordale Scar, underneath which Gray stood for a quarter of an hour – 'not without shuddering....[to depart with] an' impression that will last for life'.

Johnson, no great advocate for Gray's verse, nevertheless said of his travel writing: 'He that reads his epistolary narrative wishes that to travel, and to tell his travels, had been more his employment'.

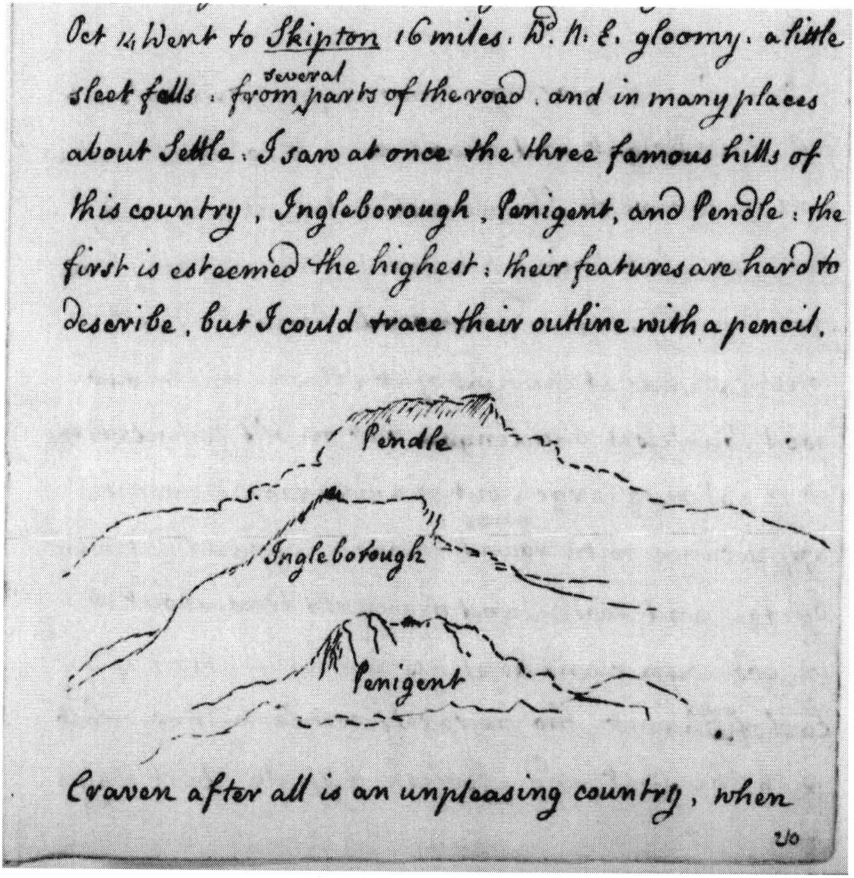

Oct 14 Went to Skipton 16 miles. Wd. N. E. gloomy. a little sleet falls: from several parts of the road, and in many places about Settle. I saw at once the three famous hills of this country, Ingleborough, Penigent, and Pendle: the first is esteemed the highest: their features are hard to describe, but I could trace their outline with a pencil.

Craven after all is an unpleasing country, when

210

An example of Gray's Handwriting from a Letter to Wharton
[British Library MSS]

[No authentic representation of Charles Victor de Bonstetten exists]

CHAPTER TWENTY-THREE

1769 November: **Bonstetten** arrives in Cambridge
1770 January to March: Cambridge
March to April: London
April to May: Thrapston and Lovingland (Lowestoft).
May : Cambridge
May : London
Early June: Cambridge
June: Aston.
June to July: Cambridge.
July to August: Tour of Wye Valley
August: London.
August to following January: Cambridge.

The overwhelming event for Gray of late November 1769 to early 1770 was the arrival in Cambridge of Charles-Victor de Bonstetten. The young Swiss aristocrat came with a letter of introduction from Norton Nicholls, whom he had met under extraordinary circumstances in Bath[59]. Aged 24, he was not the fresh-faced youth that some commentators have assumed him to be; he had already had a varied life of changing homes and experimenting with new opinions and philosophies. He was the son a wealthy Swiss diplomat, who wanted to control his son and keep him out of trouble. His adolescent years had been spent in the home of a kindly Swiss family at Yverdon but he had known no real stable home-life and certainly no maternal influence. He had come under the influence of Rousseau and had met Voltaire and espoused liberal, if not actual revolutionary opinions. Indeed, his biographer, Aimy Steinlen, makes clear that he had worshipped Voltaire in the way that he was soon to adopt towards Gray[60]. 'Quel n'est pas sur la jeunesse le prestige d'un talent superieur!

---

[59] Apparently Bonstetten had to be rescued from the gaming tables at Bath by Thomas Pitt, brother of the prime minister, who lent him his purse. He met Nicholls by climbing on to a table top to get a better view!

[60] Aimé Steinlen, *Étude Biographique etc.*, Lausanne, 1860, p. 19.'How powerful is the prestige of a superior intellect over a young man! Before this scraggy old man, who, from his retreat, carried so much weight over his century, Bonstetten was captivated'.

En face du maigre veillard qui, de sa retraite, pesait sur son siècle, Bonstetten était subjugué.' Steinlen also speaks of his gaiety and he must have had a quality of ingenuous charm, that Gray quickly found attractive. Once thrown together, the relationship developed from adulation into infatuation. According to Gosse, 'The ebullient young Swiss conquered the shy and solitary poet at sight. 'My gaiety, my love for English poetry, appeared to have subdued him....and the difference in age between us seemed to disappear at once'. Gray found him a lodging close to Pembroke Hall, at a coffee house, and at once set himself to plan for Bonstetten a course of studies....For three months the young Swiss despising all other society to be found at Cambridge, spent every evening with Gray, arriving at five o'clock, and lingering till midnight....' (Gosse, op. cit., p.196). And so it continued until late in March the following year when Bonstetten, at his father's command, tore himself away and departed for Switzerland. Gray's excitement in the relationship is clear from the letter he wrote to Bonstetten shortly after his return to Switzerland in April (Letter dated April 19, 1770).

> Alas! how do I every moment feel the truth of what I have somewhere read: *Ce n'est pas le voir que de souvenir,* and yet that remembrance is the only satisfaction I have left. My life now is but a perpetual conversation with your shadow. - The known sound of your voice still rings in my ears. - There, on the corner of the fender, you are standing, or tinkling on the Pianoforte, or stretch'd at length on the sofa. - Do you reflect, my dearest Friend, that it is a week or eight days, before I can receive a letter from you and as much more before you can have my answer, that all that time (with more than Herculean toil) I am employ'd in pushing the tedious hours along, and wishing to annihilate them; the more I strive, the heavier they move and the longer they grow. I can not bear this place, where I have spent many tedious years within leſs than a month, since you left me. I am going for a few days to see poor Nicholls invited by a letter, wherein he mentions you in such terms, as add to my regard for him, and expreſs my own sentiments better than I can do myself. 'I am concern'd (says

he) that I can not paſs my life without him, I never met with any one that pleased and suited me so well: the miracle to me, is how he comes to be so little spoil'd, and the miracle of miracles will be, if he continues so in the midst of every danger and seduction, and without any advantages, but from his own excellent nature and understanding. I own I am very anxious for him on this account, and perhaps your inquietude may have proceeded from the same cause. I hope, I am to hear, when he has paſs'd that cursed sea, or he will forget me thus *in insulam relegatum*? If he should, it is out of my power to retaliate'.

Sure you have wrote to him, my dear Bonstetten, or sure you will! he has mov'd me with these gentle and sensible expreſsions of his kindneſs for you. Are you untouch'd by them?

You do me the credit (and false or true, it goes to my heart) of ascribing to me your love for many virtues of the highest rank. Would to heaven it were so; but they are indeed the fruits of your own noble and generous understanding, that has hitherto struggled against the stream of custom, paſsion, and ill company, even when you were but a Child, and will you now give way to that stream, when your strength is increased? Shall the Jargon of French Sophists, the allurements of painted women, *comme il faut*, or the vulgar careſses of prostitute beauty, the property of all, that can afford to purchase it,, induce you to give up a mind and body by nature distinguish'd from all others to folly, disease, and vain remorse? Have a care, my ever-amiable Friend, *of loving what you do not approve*, and know me for your most faithful and most humble Despote.

Bonstetten must have been hurt by the warnings about getting involved with prostitutes and the threatening prospect of remorse and disease. This extraordinary letter - demonstrating Gray's idealistic infatuation with the young Bonstetten - was not in the selection originally published by Mason, not apparently from any misgivings on Mason's part, but because Bonstetten refused permission to Mason to print it. It later appeared, with Bonstetten's approval, in German, and was then translated back (*Letters written from various parts of the Continent Translated from the German of Frederick Matthison*, Anne Plumptree, London 1799). Gray's love for this undoubtedly handsome and talented young man was passionate and overwhelming - nothing wrong with that, except in so far as it became possessive.

There were after-shocks following the four-month emotional earthquake that Bonstetten had triggered - but not many, and they soon subsided. Gray made efforts to obtain a portrait of Bonstetten, but when it came, he found it disappointing. Nicholls tried to arrange a visit to Berne for himself and Gray but it came to nothing. Bonstetten never forgot Gray, however, and his verdict on the encounter, written sixty years later, is interesting. 'Je crois que Gray n'avait jamais aimé, c'était le mot de l'énigme.'[61] He went on to perform a number of minor political and diplomatic roles and to write some fairly unrewarding works of observational literature. He died in 1832.

Some commentators have found it difficult to explain this event in Gray's life. Ketton-Cremer, for instance, saw it as an out-of-character once-in-a lifetime inexplicable mental adventure. The following comment was the best he could do in the way of explanation: 'Gray's health was gradually failing, and the strength of his affection for Bonstetten exhausted and perturbed him. He had excluded strong personal emotion from his life; and now, in his last years, he was puzzled and bewildered to find that he could be so deeply moved'. Later critics have found it less difficult to come to terms with what had happened. Raymond Bentman, for instance, writes of 'the unmistakable amorousness' of Gray's letters[62]. His verdict is that Gray was homosexual in orientation but that he was compelled, in an age of legal persecution, to suppress his feelings. Roger Lonsdale, without being so explicit, came to a similar conclusion. 'This one, sad, unignorable exposure of the heart does not provide us with a key which unlocks the secret of Gray's poetry. Yet it may suggest why his poetic career as

[61] *Souvenirs de Ch. Victor de Bonstetten* (1831), pp.116-119, quoted in Works of Gray, Vol V, p.181.

[62] Raymond Bentman, *Thomas Gray and the Poetry of "Hopeless Love"*, Journal of the History of Sexuality, Vol. 3/2, 1992, pp.203-222.

a whole had become a process of escape from a dimly understood sense of a private predicament, which was in itself the real spring of his creativity.'[63] Roger Martin, as probably the first to face up to this assessment, comes to an even more striking conclusion: 'il mourut l'an d'apres, miné peut-être par son torment'. It is not necessary to go so far. Gradually, in Martin's words, 'La brulante passion s'éteignit'['The burning passion burnt itself out']. But he did need to get away. It is arguable that the trip to the Wye valley brought him back to his old self, that he regained his poise and settled back into the compromise, the suppression, which had got him through the turbulence of his emotional life.

[63] Roger Lonsdale, Proceedings of the British Academy, *The Poetry of Thomas Gray: versions of the Self*, 21 Feb 1973, p. 122/3.

A View of New Weir on the River Wye,
Engraving by Francis Jukes after Edward Dayes, c. 180

CHAPTER TWENTY-FOUR

1770 January to March: Cambridge
March**: Bonstetten** leaves
March to April: London
April to May: Thrapston and Lovingland (Lowestoft).
May : Cambridge
May : London
Early June: Cambridge
June: Aston.
June to July: Cambridge.
July to August: Tour of Wye Valley
August: London.
August to following January: Cambridge.

After the departure of Bonstetten, Gray needed constant movement: Cambridge to London to Cambridge to London to Aston. He returned from Aston towards the end of June, and prepared at once to start with Norton Nicholls for a summer tour. He directed Nicholls to meet him at the sign of the Wheat Sheaf, five miles beyond Huntingdon, about the 3rd July. Unfortunately there exists no journal to commemorate this, the last of Gray's tours, which seems to have occupied more than two months. All we have is the following letter from Gray to Wharton, written from Cambridge on his return in August 1770.

My dear Doctor

I am lately return'd from a six weeks ramble through Worcestershire, Gloucestershire, Monmouthsh: Herefordsh: & Shropshire, five of the most beautiful counties in the kingdom. the very light, & principal feature in my journey was the river Wye, wch I descended in a boat for nearly 40 miles from Ross to Chepstow: its banks are a succeſsion of nameleſs wonders: one out of many you may see not ill described by Mr. Whateley in his *Observations on Gardening* under the name of the New-Weir: he has also touch'd upon two others, *Tinterne Abbey*, and *Persfield* (Mr Morris's), both of them famous scenes; & both on the Wye. Monmouth, a town I never heard mention'd, lies on the same river in a vale, that is the delight of my eyes, & the very seat of pleasure. the vale of Abergavenny, Ragland & Chepstow-Castles, Ludlow, Malvern-hills, Hampton-Court near Lemster[64], the Leasowes, Hagley, the three Cities & their Cathedrals, & lastly Oxford (where I past two days in my return with great satisfaction), are the rest of my acquisitions, & no bad harvest to my thinking. I have a journal written by the companion of my travels[65], that serves to recall & fix the fading images of these things.

I desire to hear of your health, & that of your family. are Miss Wh: & Miss Peggy quite recover'd? my respects to Mrs Wharton & them.

I am ever Yours, T: G: Pemb: Coll: Aug: 24 1770

One of the major undiscovered mystery manuscripts of the long eighteenth-century must be this journal, referred to here by Gray, of his travels down the Wye with his friend, Norton Nicholls. 'I have a journal written by the companion of my travels,that serves to recall & fix the fading images of these things'. One must assume from these words that the two of them kept a diary of a journey of considerable length through some of the major tourist sites that were beginning to attract attention in the final quarter of the eighteenth century: not only the Wye itself as a river journey through both wild landscape and cultivated estates, but the Malvern hills and other pilgrimage sites such as Leasowes. As Gray says, this was quite a haul - ' no bad harvest' - for one expedition. The journal may well remain undiscovered, since the obvious places for its survival have revealed nothing. Norton Nicholls' will speaks of his

[64] Leominster, in Herefordshire. This Hampton Court was the seat of the Coningsby family.

[65] Norton Nicholls.

bequeathing his Gray papers to Thomas Mathias. Thomas Mathias in his turn left his library and papers to be sold in the 1850's, with no mention in the catalogue of anything sounding like a journal. It would not be difficult, however, given the nature of the old exercise books that Gray used on previous tours to Scotland and the Lakes, for such an unprepossessing document either to be thrown away or to be still lingering, un-remarked and un-catalogued in a box in an attic or a cupboard at a solicitor's, or thrown with other papers in a 'miscellaneous' folder in a record office. One can therefore still keep hoping, and searching.

The condition of the valley that Gray passed through then was distinctly different then from the experience it offers now. Tintern Abbey was and is the central point but it has, inevitably, been tidied up, with fences and floodlights, regularly mown grass, interpretation boards, and so on. This has not quite killed the beauty of the setting and it was still an experience to hear Wordsworth's poem recited one warm summer's night from the nave of the ruined arches.

> Once again
> Do I behold these steep and lofty cliffs,
> That on a wild secluded scene impress
> Thoughts of more deep seclusion....

In Gray's day, and in Gilpin's at about the same time, the experience was mixed with the sounds of the hammers of a nearby forge and the smoke from its furnaces drifting across. The foundations of the forge remain, up a side valley, not far from the abbey, and it is being rescued by keen archaeologists. It is the same mixture of experience that Gray had come across on his Lakes tour near Sizergh: 'the thumping of huge hammers at an iron forge not ar distant made it a singular walk'. Piercefield, which Gray mentions, and not far distant down river, was then laid out with woodland walks, grottos, caves and temples. The house is now derelict and it is hard to feel any enthusiasm for the muddle that is left.

Gray quotes, with qualified approval ('not ill described'), Whatelely's *Observations on Modern Gardening* (London, 1770) on this stretch of the river. Whatelely describes Tintern in some detail; 'the original construction of the church is perfectly marked', but while he admires the state of preservation he appears also to admire its covering by 'tufts of ivy' and 'lighter foliage', asking only that it be kept 'clear from weeds and bushes'. It is evident that at the end of the eighteenth century they liked their ruins to look neglected! Whately goes on from his description of Tintern to recommending the erection of 'fictitious ruins': 'all certain, but all in decay; and suggesting, at once, every idea which can occur in a seat of devotion, solitude, and desolation'. This is a formidable recommendation of ruin for the sake of ruin, of follies to decorate the view, and of the Ossianic mood of melancholy in solitude - an end-of-century style of the picturesque with which Gray probably sympathized. If they liked their ruins to look ruined, they were also not at all averse to smoke and the noise of machinery, to the excitement of industrialization alongside their discovery of wild nature. Whateley enjoys this union of the industrial and the scenic in his enthusiastic, mannered, and lengthy description of another pilgrimage site on the Wye, New Weir[66].

> A scene at the New Weir on the Wye, which in itself is truly great and awful, so far from from being disturbed, becomes more interesting and important, by the business to which it is destined. It is a chasm between two high ranges of hill, which rise almost perpendicularly from the water, the rocks on the sides are mostly heavy masses and their colour is generally brown ; but here and there a pale craggy shape starts up to a vast heighth above the rest, unconnected, broken, and bare: large trees frequently force out their way amongst them; and many of them stand far back in the covert, where their natural dusky hue is deepened by the shadow which overhangs them. The river too, as it retires, loses itself in woods which close immediately above, then rise thick and high, and darken the water. In the midst of all this gloom is an iron forge, covered with a black cloud of smoak, and surrounded with half-burned ore, with coal, and with cinders; the fuel for it is brought down a path, worn into steps, narrow and steep, and winding among precipices ; and near it is an open space of barren moor, about which are scattered the huts of the workmen. It

[66] Near a place now called Symonds's Yat, between Ross and Monmouth.

> stands close to the cascade of the Weir, where the agitation of the current is encreased by large fragments of rocks, which have been swept down by floods from the banks, or shivered by tempests from the brow and the sullen sound, at stated intervals, from the strokes of the great hammers in the forge, deadens the roar of the water-fall. Just below it, while the rapidity of the stream still continues, a ferry is carried across it; and lower down the fishermen use little round boats, called truckles[67], the remains perhaps of the ancient British navigation, which the least motion will overset, and the slightest touch may destroy. All the employments of the people seem to require either exertion or caution , and the ideas of force or of danger which attend them, give to the scene an animation unknown to a solitary, though perfectly compatible with the wildest romantic situations.

Gray's missing journal was survived by its twin, a journal kept by William Gilpin of a tour of the Wye, made at almost the same time as Gray's. In the Preface, Gilpin makes the following apologia: 'In the same year in which this little journey was made, Mr Gray made it likewise; and hearing that I had put on paper a few remarks on the scenes, which he had so lately visited, he desired a sight of them. They were then only in a rude state; but the handsome things he said of them to a friend of his [William Fraser] who obligingly repeated them to me, gave them, I own, some little degree of credit in my opinion; and made me less apprehensive in risking them before the public'. Gilpin must have delayed somewhat in going to press but print he did and the result was a typically wordy Gilpin title, *Observations on the River Wye and several parts of South Wales, &c. relating chiefly to Picturesque Beauty made in the Summer of the year 1770.*

Gilpin's book is short but full of interest, sometimes for the wrong reasons. For example, his remarks on Tintern Abbey are so extraordinary as to demand verbatim inclusion [the bold type is mine]:

[67] A curious word which can mean a cheese, a bed, to yield, or, as here, a wicker-work boat, still in use amongst Welsh fishermen and on the Irish lakes.

> No part of the ruins of Tintern is seen from the river, except the abbey-church. It has been an elegant Gothic pile ; but it does not make that appearance as a distant object, which we expected. Tho' the parts are beautiful, the whole is ill-shaped. No ruins of the tower are left, which might give form, and contrast to the buttresses, and walls. Instead of this, a number of gable-ends hurt the eye with their regularity ; and disgust it by the vulgarity of their shape. **A mallet judiciously used** (but who durst use it ?) might be of service in fracturing some of them ; particularly those of the cross aisles, which are both disagreeable in themselves, and confound the perspective.

Gilpin also leaves himself open to satirical comment on a different count, in his complaints about the weather.

> I must however premise, how ill-qualified I am to do justice to the banks of the Wye, were it only from having seen them under the circumstance of a continued rain ; which began early in the day, before one third of our voyage was performed.

Gilpin, like Whateley, also came out in favour of a little industrial smog, giving a pleasing haze to the view:

> Many of the furnaces, on the banks of the river, consume charcoal, which is manufactured on the spot ; and the smoke, issuing from the sides of the hills; and spreading it's thin veil over a part of them, beautifully breaks their lines, and unites them with the sky.

Gilpin is also frequently wooden and methodical in his descriptive method, reducing the appreciation of wild scenery to a set of rules: "The ornaments of the Wye may be ranged under four heads: ground, wood, rock, and buildings." What upset Gilpin, however, indeed completely threw him, in the modern phrase, was a sudden and unexpected shock of reality in the shape of extreme poverty. It breaks the aura of scenic romanticism so sedulously created and introduces a note of Cobbett-like rural destitution.

> One poor woman we followed, who had engaged to shew us the monk's library. She could scarce crawl; shuffling along her palsied limbs, and meagre, contracted body, by the help of two sticks. She led us, through an old gate, into a place over spread with nettles, and briars ; and pointing to the remnant of a shattered cloisler, told us, that was the place. It was her own mansion. All indeed she meant to tell us, was the story of her own wretchedness ; and all she had to shew us was her own miserable habitation. We did not expect to be interested : but we found we were. I never saw so loathsome a human dwelling.

For all that, Gilpin's was an influential voice and many tourists followed him to the Wye valley, with his book in their luggage. At least he 'roughed' it in an open boat with a crew of three to pole it down the river through stretches of rough water, in contrast to the launches with powerful outboards and fridges full of ice-cream and cup-cakes that do the journey now. It was still something of an adventure on the water.

We can only speculate on what Gray would have written, or on what he did write and we have so far lost. From the evidence of the Scottish and Lake District journals, it would have been more spirited, more metaphorical, a more poetic prose than Gilpin or Whatelely.

Gray's tomb (left) at Stoke Poges Church
[Photograph in public domain]

CHAPTER TWENTY-FIVE

1771 .January: London.
January to mid-May: Cambridge.
May 16 - July 22: London.
July 22 - 30: Cambridge (Dies July 30)

Gray should not have died at the relatively young age of 55. He was a man of delicate health, fussy about his health, but not constitutionally weak. He had, it is true, been a valetudinarian for most of his life, watching his health, complaining to friends, making notes in his diaries and notebooks of pains and upsets. Like many hypochondriacs, he was addicted to self-medication, using his friend Dr Wharton for supplementary advice. There is a long passage in an earlier letter (To Wharton, Jan. 9, 1756) where he describes taking soap, presumably for some stomach or laxative complaint. Awful to think about it but better than the lime-water which Wharton has also apparently recommended. No--one dies of hypochondria and many hypochondriacs live to ripe old age. No reason why Gray should not have done so for, although slight in build, he had a reasonably strong physical constitution. He had, the previous year, carried out a strenuous tour, which included climbing the Herefordshire Beacon, and was at the height of his mental powers. There is no sign that he felt that he had come to the end of what he had to do. (It is worth remembering that Cowper was 68 when he wrote his finest poem, *The Castaway*). He had no serious bad habits of over-eating or over-drinking and was careful, indeed particular, over his diet. In 1764 he had had a bad attack of Piles and had needed surgery, always a risky affair in those days. His pocket-book for 1755 has occasional notes in Latin: *pectoris oppressio &dolor* and *nox turbida capitis* - one way of complaining, without letting anyone-else know. He did, however, suffer from occasional periods of what he called gout and in June of 1771 he seems to have had a bad attack of an undiagnosed liver or stomach complaint. In the twenty-first century he would have been packed off to hospital, been subjected to a battery of tests, possibly had some minor operation, and been out again within days. Eighteenth-century medicine being what it was and varying considerably from doctor to doctor, Gray's condition was neglected and he was left to grow worse. He wrote two letters in his final days, both from London, where he had been advised to rest.

The first was to his Cambridge colleague, James Brown, on June 22nd.

> I write just to tell you the reason of my stay here. The gout has left me, but I have a feverish disorder, that seems to return regularly upon me every morning, & leaves me very weak and spiritless. another complaint has come upon me yesterday, that makes me unfit to bear the journey to Cambridge. Dr Gisbourne advises me to take a lodging at Kensington for a week or two, & I believe I shall try this expedient to morrow. my illness has prevented me from doing anything about your carpet, wch I hope you will excuse. pray write to me & direct as usual in Jermyn Street.
>
> I am ever, Yours T:G:

If Gray was worrying about James Brown's carpet, he would not seem to be aware of the possible seriousness of his illness. In the last letter that he wrote, however, a few days later from lodgings in Jermyn Street, London to his young friend, Norton Nicholls, he was clearly more worried.

> Dear S^{r}
> The inclosed came a few days after you left us, as I apprehend, from Temple. I continue here much against my will. the gout is gone, the feverish disorder abated, but not cured; my spirits much oppressed, & the more so, as I foresee a new complaint, that may tie me down perhaps to my bed, & expose me to the operations of a Surgeon. God knows what will be the end of it....

These two letters are the last that Gray wrote. He appears to have stayed in London a few weeks longer but then decided that if he was going to be ill, he would rather be in Cambridge. On 22nd July he returned to Cambridge. He did not improve. On July 26th Brown wrote to Nicholls with the latest report. 'His illness is something like the Gout in the Stomach but as Dr Glyn tells me there are many different degrees of that disorder, we may hope this is one of the less dangerous degrees, and that we shall see him well again in a short time...' By the 29th, however, that hope seems to have suddenly evaporated. Brown wrote to Wharton: 'Poor Mr Gray! my dear S^r I am afraid his friends at Old Park will see him no more. Professor Plumptree and Dr Glynn give us no hope of his recovery, they both attend him, and come together three or four times a day. They say it is the Gout in the Stomach, & they cannot get the better of it....' On the evening of July 30 Gray was clearly dying and on the 31st Brown wrote again to Wharton. 'You must expect what will give you great concern; Mr Gray died about eleven last night; there is nothing to be added about his death but that the whole was peaceable and calm....'

Gray appears to have died from kidney failure. Whibley in the *Correspondence* quotes a Sir Humphrey Rolleston as concluding that the illness was chronic kidney disease, terminating in uraemia[68]. But it is impossible to know now quite what it was that killed Gray. There are plenty of commentators ready to be critical of the doctor who attended Gray, a Dr Glynn, 'conspicuous for his gold-headed cane, scarlet coat, three-cornered hat, and resounding pattens', according to Gosse. At least Stephen Hempsted, Gray's valet, comes out of the story of the last days with some credit; according to Brown, 'Stephen, his old servant is very diligent and handy in his attendance upon him'. [It is good to know that Gray remembered Stephen in his will: 'I give to my servant... fifty pounds....and all my wearing apparel & linnen']. Modern medicine no doubt would have kept Gray alive.

In his will, Gray asked to be buried in the vault 'made by my late dear Mother in the churchyard at Stoke Pogeis....in a coffin of season'd oak neither lined nor cover'd'. This says something about Gray's beliefs, at a time when it was common for coffins to be lead-lined, to preserve the body for its resurrection. No doubt he would be flattered to know that his tomb was to be renovated three hundred years later. Gray, who was moderately wealthy by the time of his death (no thanks to publisher's royalties), left the bulk of his estate to his cousin, Mary Antrobus, with generous legacies to his friends, Richard

---

68 Page 1272, note 2. Humphrey Rolleston (1862-1944) was a prominent English physician, at St George's Hospital London and physician-in-ordinary to King George V.

Stonehewer, Thomas Wharton, William Mason, and James Brown. William Mason, in particular, was appointed his literary executor, with a charge over all his 'books, manuscripts, musick, and papers of all kinds to preserve or destroy at his own discretion'.

Gray's Monument in Poet's Corner, Westminster Abbey
(Photograph by courtesy of Westminster Abbey)

CONCLUSION

GRAY'S REPUTATION

Gray remains the poet of *The Elegy*. But there are other dimensions, depths, hidden qualities. He is, in particular, more human than has been granted him, more considerate, more generous, to an admittedly small circle of interesting friends. He is more versatile, more interested in natural history, in travel, in contemporary events, in people. He is less timid, more enterprising, more physically active, more original and more adventurous in poetic styles and forms. He is also more remarkable for his command of languages, for his range of cultural interests, for his ability to read in depth.

Gray wrote one poem with a readership far in excess of any other literary work of the century . He achieved a reputation and fame equal to, or greater than, that of Johnson, Pope, Thompson, Cowper, a status hidden from us by his current inexplicable lack of popularity. Why is it then that so few research students choose to work on his achievements, why is it that there is no Gray Society holding annual meetings and conferences and journals, why is his work not prescribed in national exam syllabi, why have most bookshops none, or at least few, of his works on their shelves?

Partly, it is because Gray is thought of as identifying with the conventional, with an uninteresting premier division of English Literature, with an upper-class culture and economic status, with a historical connection with empire and aristocratic power structure, with an educational bias towards the uncontroversial, the out-of-date corpus of respectable classics. Far more interesting surely to ferret among the unknown, minor, preferably female, poets and writers of working-class backgrounds, of Irish or Welsh origins, of wayward sexual orientation if possible, unpublished and undiscovered.

What chance is there then of marketing a warmly human Gray, with a liking for domestic life and a penchant for enterprising travel, whose achievement was to open up the whole field of Romanticism, who ventured into new forms of writing and opened our eyes into new kinds of experience in wild countryside. Wordsworth may now have the glory but Gray got there first, in his lonely, courageous, and ultimately tragic excursus into the unknown, Gray was the true, the first revolutionary.

Gray's popularity was at its height just after his death, when Mason commissioned the memorial to him which is now to be found in Poet's Corner in Westminster Abbey. It is a telling index of his unpopularity now that when I went to Westminster Abbey and asked after the memorial, not one of the guides had heard of Thomas Gray, and when I did track down the memorial, I found it to be almost completely invisible, hidden behind a stack of chairs. Gray would not realise - or perhaps he would - how ironic would be the lines in the *Elegy:*

> Yet ev'n these bones from insult to protect,
> Some frail memorial still erected nigh,
> With uncouth rhymes and speechless sculpture deck'd
> Implores the passing tribute of a sigh.

A Note on the Illustrations

Two of the illustrations are my own photographs; two are in the public domain. The rest are taken with permission from the British Museum Collection database. This allows the use of images for non-commercial and academic purposes, providing they are accompanied by an acknowledgement: © The Trustees of the British Museum. I am grateful to be allowed the use of this extensive source of material.